PENGUIN MODERN CLASSICS

R. S. Thomas: Selected Poems

Ronald Stuart Thomas was born in Cardiff in 1913, and grew up in Ynys Mon (Anglesey), where he returned at the end of his life. He read Classics at University College Bangor, North Wales, and was ordained as a priest in 1937. For the next forty years, he worked as a parish priest in the Church of Wales. In 1940 he married the artist M. E. Eldridge and they had one son. Thomas's first volume of poetry, *The Stones of the Field*, appeared in 1946. Despite shunning literary and academic circles, his poetry reflects a passionate engagement with the major concerns and discourses of the twentieth century – technology and science, machines, ecology and the natural environment, the family, language, the problem of pain and suffering – as well as a continuing dialogue with a God who is now present and accessible through prayer and now absent and uncommunicative. He is considered by many to have been the greatest religious poet writing in English in the last century. He published fifty books of poetry, including *Song at the Year's Turning* (1955), *Tares* (1961), *Laboratories of the Spirit* (1976), *Mass for Hard Times* (1992) and *No Truce with the Furies* (1995), the last volume to appear during his lifetime, together with prose in Welsh, the language he learned as an adult.

Thomas's work has been translated and published in all the major European languages as well as Chinese and Japanese. He won numerous prizes, including the Heinemann Award in 1955, the Cheltenham prize in 1963, the Queen's Gold Medal for poetry in 1964 and the Cholmondeley Award in 1978. He received three Welsh Arts Council Literature Awards, and was nominated for the Nobel Prize for Literature in 1994. His autobiography, *Neb (No one)*, was published in Welsh in 1985. He died in 2000.

R. S. THOMAS

Selected Poems

PENGUIN BOOKS

PENGUIN BOOKS

Published by the Penguin Group

Penguin Books Ltd, 80 Strand, London WC2R 0RL, England

Penguin Group (USA) Inc., 375 Hudson Street, New York 10014, USA

Penguin Books Australia Ltd, 250 Camberwell Road, Camberwell, Victoria 3124, Australia

Penguin Books Canada Ltd, 10 Alcorn Avenue, Toronto, Ontario, Canada M4V 3B2

Penguin Books India (P) Ltd, 11 Community Centre, Panchsheel Park, New Delhi – 110 017, India

Penguin Books (NZ) Ltd, Cnr Rosedale and Airborne Roads, Albany, Auckland, New Zealand

Penguin Books (South Africa) (Pty) Ltd, 24 Sturdee Avenue, Rosebank 2196, South Africa

Penguin Books Ltd, Registered Offices: 80 Strand, London WC2R 0RL, England

www.penguin.com

This selection first published 2003

024

Copyright © 1946, 1952, 1953, 1955, 1958, 1961, 1963, 1966, 1968, 1972, 1973, 1974, 1975, 1977, 1978, 1981, 1983, 1985, 1986, 1987, 1988, 1990, 1992, 1995, 2004 by R. S. Thomas

Selected Poems 1946–1968, first published 1973 by Granada Publishing, copyright © R. S. Thomas
Later Poems, first published 1983 by Macmillan London Limited, copyright © R. S. Thomas 1972, 1974, 1975, 1977, 1978, 1981, 1983
Experimenting with an Amen, first published 1986 by Macmillan London Limited, copyright © R. S. Thomas, 1986
Welsh Airs, first published 1987 by Poetry Wales Press, copyright © R. S. Thomas
The Echoes Return Slow, first published 1988 by Macmillan London Limited, copyright © R. S. Thomas 1988
Counterpoint, first published 1990 by Bloodaxe Books Ltd, copyright © R. S. Thomas 1990
Mass for Hard Times, first published 1992 by Bloodaxe Books Ltd, copyright © R. S. Thomas 1992
Collected Poems, 1945–1990, first published by J. M. Dent in 1993, copyright © R. S. Thomas 1993
No Truce with the Furies, first published 1995 by Bloodaxe Books Ltd, copyright © R. S. Thomas 1995
Unpublished poems copyright © Rhodri Thomas 2004
All rights reserved

The moral right of the author has been asserted

Set in 10/12.5 pt Monotype Garamond
Typeset by Rowland Phototypesetting Ltd, Bury St Edmunds, Suffolk

Printed and bound in Great Britain by Clays Ltd, Elcograf S.p.A.

ISBN-13: 978-0-14-018890-5

www.greenpenguin.co.uk

Contents

Contents

Contents

Contents

from *No Truce With the Furies* 1995

Unpublished Poems

Contents

from *The Stones of the Fields* 1946

A Peasant

Iago Prytherch his name, though, be it allowed,
Just an ordinary man of the bald Welsh hills,
Who pens a few sheep in a gap of cloud.
Docking mangels, chipping the green skin
From the yellow bones with a half-witted grin
Of satisfaction, or churning the crude earth
To a stiff sea of clouds that glint in the wind –
So are his days spent, his spittled mirth
Rarer than the sun that cracks the cheeks
Of the gaunt sky perhaps once in a week.
And then at night see him fixed in his chair
Motionless, except when he leans to gob in the fire.
There is something frightening in the vacancy of his mind.
His clothes, sour with years of sweat
And animal contact, shock the refined,
But affected, sense with their stark naturalness.
Yet this is your prototype, who, season by season
Against siege of rain and the wind's attrition,
Preserves his stock, an impregnable fortress
Not to be stormed even in death's confusion.
Remember him, then, for he, too, is a winner of wars,
Enduring like a tree under the curious stars.

The Cry of Elisha after Elijah

The chariot of Israel came,
And the bold, beautiful knights,
To free from his close prison
The friend who was my delight;
Cold is my cry over the vast deep shaken,
Bereft was I, for he was taken.

Through the straight places of Baca
We went with an equal will,
Not knowing who would emerge
First from that gloomy vale;
Cold is my cry; our bond was broken,
Bereft was I, for he was taken.

Where, then, came they to rest,
Those steeds and that car of fire?
My understanding is darkened,
It is no gain to enquire;
Better to await the long night's ending,
Till the light comes, far truths transcending.

I yield, since no wisdom lies
In seeking to go his way;
A man without knowledge am I
Of the quality of his joy;
Yet living souls, a prodigious number,
Bright-faced as dawn, invest God's chamber.

The friends that we loved well,
Though they vanished far from our sight,
In a new country were found
Beyond this vale of night;
O blest are they, without pain or fretting
In the sun's light that knows no setting.
   (*From the Welsh of Thomas Williams,*
   Bethesda'r Fro)

Song

Wandering, wandering, hoping to find
The ring of mushrooms with the wet rind,
Cold to the touch, but bright with dew,
A green asylum from time's range.

And finding instead the harsh ways
Of the ruinous wind and the clawed rain;
The storm's hysteria in the bush;
The wild creatures and their pain.

from *An Acre of Land* 1952

Welsh Landscape

To live in Wales is to be conscious
At dusk of the spilled blood
That went to the making of the wild sky,
Dyeing the immaculate rivers
In all their courses.
It is to be aware,
Above the noisy tractor
And hum of the machine
Of strife in the strung woods,
Vibrant with sped arrows.
You cannot live in the present,
At least not in Wales.
There is the language for instance,
The soft consonants
Strange to the ear.
There are cries in the dark at night
As owls answer the moon,
And thick ambush of shadows,
Hushed at the fields' corners.
There is no present in Wales,
And no future;
There is only the past,
Brittle with relics,
Wind-bitten towers and castles
With sham ghosts;

Mouldering quarries and mines;
And an impotent people,
Sick with inbreeding,
Worrying the carcase of an old song.

The Minister 1953

Characters
NARRATOR   The Minister
DAVIES   Buddug

NARRATOR
In the hill country at the moor's edge
There is a chapel, religion's outpost
In the untamed land west of the valleys,
The marginal land where flesh meets spirit
Only on Sundays and the days between
Are mortgaged to the grasping soil.

This is the land of green hay
And greener corn, because of the long
Tarrying of winter and the late spring.
This is the land where they burn peat
If there is time for cutting it,
And the weather improves for drying it,
And the cart is not too old for carrying it
And doesn't get stuck in the wet bog.

This is the land where men labour
In silence, and the rusted harrow
Breaks its teeth on the grey stones.
Below, the valleys are an open book,
Bound in sunlight; but the green tale
Told in its pages is not true.

'Beloved, let us love one another,' the words are blown
To pieces by the unchristened wind
In the chapel rafters, and love's text
Is riddled by the inhuman cry
Of buzzards circling above the moor.
Come with me, and we will go
Back through the darkness of the vanished years
To peer inside through the low window
Of the chapel vestry, the bare room
That is sour with books and wet clothes.

They chose their pastors as they chose their horses
For hard work. But the last one died
Sooner than they expected; nothing sinister,
You understand, but just the natural
Breaking of the heart beneath a load
Unfit for horses. 'Ay, he's a good 'un,'
Job Davies had said; and Job was a master
Hand at choosing a nag or a pastor.

And Job was right, but he forgot,
They all forgot that even a pastor
Is a man first and a minister after,
Although he wears the sober armour
Of God, and wields the fiery tongue
Of God, and listens to the voice
Of God, the voice no others listen to;
The voice that is the well-kept secret
Of man, like Santa Claus,
Or where baby came from;
The secret waiting to be told
When we are older and can stand the truth.

O, but God is in the throat of a bird;
Ann heard Him speak, and Pantycelyn.
God is in the sound of the white water

Falling at Cynfal. God is in the flowers
Sprung at the feet of Olwen, and Melangell
Felt His heart beating in the wild hare.
Wales in fact is His peculiar home,
Our fathers knew Him. But where is that voice now?
Is it in the chapel vestry, where Davies is using
The logic of the Smithfield?

DAVIES

A young 'un we want, someone young
Without a wife. Let him learn
His calling first, and choose after
Among our girls, if he must marry.
There's your girl, Pugh; or yours, Parry;
Ministers' wives they ought to be
With those white hands that are too soft
For lugging muck or pulling a cow's
Tits. But ay, he must be young.

Remember that mare of yours, John?

Too old when you bought her; the old sinner
Had had a taste of the valleys first
And never took to the rough grass
In the top fields. You could do nothing
With her, but let her go her way.
Lucky you sold her. But you can't sell
Ministers, so we must have a care
In choosing. Take my advice,
Pick someone young, and I'll soon show him
How things is managed in the hills here.

NARRATOR

Did you notice the farm on the hill side
A bit larger than the others, a bit more hay
In the Dutch barn, four cows instead of two?

Prosperity is a sign of divine favour:
Whoever saw the righteous forsaken
Or his seed begging their bread? It even entitles
A chapel deacon to a tame pastor.

There were people here before these,
Measuring truth according to the moor's
Pitiless commentary and the wind's veto.
Out in the moor there is a bone whitening,
Worn smooth by the long dialectic
Of rain and sunlight. What has that to do
With choosing a minister? Nothing, nothing.

Thick darkness is about us, we cannot see
The future, nor the thin face
Of him whom necessity will bring
To this lean oasis at the moor's rim,
The marginal land where flesh meets spirit
Only on Sundays and the days between
Are mortgaged, mortgaged, mortgaged.
But we can see the faces of the men
Grouped together under the one lamp,
Waiting for the name to be born to them
Out of time's heaving thighs.

Did you dream, wanderer in the night,
Of the ruined house with the one light
Shining; and that you were the moth
Drawn relentlessly out of the dark?
The room was empty, but not for long.
You thought you knew them, but they always changed
To something stranger, if you looked closely
Into their faces. And you wished you hadn't come.
You wished you were back in the wide night
Under the stars. But when you got up to go
There was a hand preventing you.

And when you tried to cry out, the cry got stuck
In your dry throat, and you lay there in travail,
Big with your cry, until the dawn delivered you
And your cry was still-born and you arose and buried it,
Laying on it wreaths of the birds' songs.
But for some there is no dawn, only the light
Of the Cross burning up the long aisle
Of night; and for some there is not even that.

The cow goes round and round the field,
Bored with its grass world, and in its eyes
The mute animal hunger, which you pity,
You the confirmed sentimentalist,
Playing the old anthropomorphic game.
But for the cow, it is the same world over the hedge.
No one ever teased her with pictures of flyless meadows,
Where the grass is eternally green
No matter how often the tongue bruises it,
Or the dung soils it.

But with man it is otherwise.
His slow wound deepens with the years,
And knows no healing only the sharp
Distemper of remembered youth.

THE MINISTER
The Reverend Elias Morgan, BA:
I am the name on whom the choice fell.
I came in April, I came young
To the hill chapel, where long hymns were sung
Three times on a Sunday, but rarely between
By a lean-faced people in black clothes,
That smelled of camphor and dried sweat.

It was the time when curlews return
To lay their eggs in the brown heather.

Their piping was the spring's cadenza
After winter's unchanging tune.
But no one heard it, they were too busy
Turning the soil and turning the minister
Over and under with the tongue's blade.

My cheeks were pale and my shoulders bowed
With years of study, but my eyes glowed
With a deep, inner pthisic zeal,
For I was the lamp which the elders chose
To thaw the darkness that had congealed
About the hearts of the hill folk.

I wore a black coat, being fresh from college,
With striped trousers, and, indeed, my knowledge
Would have been complete, had it included
The bare moor, where nature brooded
Over her old, inscrutable secret.
But I didn't even know the names
Of the birds and the flowers by which one gets
A little closer to nature's heart.

Unlike the others my house had a gate
And railings enclosing a tall bush
Of stiff cypress, which the loud thrush
Took as its pulpit early and late.
Its singing troubled my young mind
With strange theories, pagan but sweet,
That made the Book's black letters dance
To a tune John Calvin never heard.
The evening sunlight on the wall
Of my room was a new temptation.
Luther would have thrown his Bible at it.
I closed my eyes, and went on with my sermon.

NARRATOR

A few flowers bloomed beneath the window,
Set there once by a kind hand
In the old days, a woman's gesture
Of love against the childless years.
Morgan pulled them up; they were untidy.
He sprinkled cinders there instead.

Who is this opening and closing the Book
With a bang, and pointing a finger
Before him in accusation?
Who is this leaning from the wide pulpit
In judgment, and filling the chapel
With sound as God fills the sky?
Is that his shadow on the wall behind?
Shout on, Morgan. You'll be nothing tomorrow.

The people were pleased with their new pastor;
Their noses dripped and the blood ran faster
Along their veins, as the hot sparks
Fell from his lips on their dry thoughts:
The whole chapel was soon ablaze.
Except for the elders, and even they were moved
By the holy tumult, but not extremely.
They knew better than that.

It was sex, sex, sex and money, money,
God's mistake and the devil's creation,
That took the mind of the congregation
On long journeys into the hills
Of a strange land, where sin was the honey
Bright as sunlight in death's hive.
They lost the parable and found the story,
And their glands told them they were still alive.
Job looked at Buddug, and she at him

Over the pews, and they knew they'd risk it
Some evening when the moon was low.

BUDDUG

I know the place, under the hedge
In the top meadow; it was where my mam
Got into trouble, and only the stars
Were witness of the secret act.
They say her mother was the same.
Well, why not? It's hard on a girl
In these old hills, where youth is short
And boys are scarce; and the ones we'd marry
Are poor or shy. But Job's got money,
And his wife is old. Don't look at me
Like that, Job; I'm trying to listen
To what the minister says. Your eyes
Scare me, yet my bowels ache
With a strange frenzy. This is what
My mother and her mother felt
For the men who took them under the hedge.

NARRATOR

The moor pressed its face to the window.
The clock ticked on, the sermon continued.
Out in the fir-tree an owl cried
Derision on a God of love.
But no one noticed, and the voice burned on,
Consuming the preacher to a charred wick.

THE MINISTER

I was good that night, I had the *hwyl*.
We sang the verses of the last hymn
Twice. We might have had a revival
If only the organ had kept in time.
But that was the organist's fault.
I went to my house with the light heart

Of one who had made a neat job
Of pruning the branches on the tree
Of good and evil. Llywarch came with me
As far as the gate. Who was the girl
Who smiled at me as she slipped by?

NARRATOR
There was cheese for supper and cold bacon,
Or an egg if he liked; all of them given
By Job Davies as part of his pay.
Morgan sat down in his white shirt-sleeves
And cut the bacon in slices the way
His mother used to. He sauced each mouthful
With tasty memories of the day.
Supper over, can you picture him there
Slumped in his chair by the red fire
Listening to the clock's sound, shy as a mouse,
Pattering to and fro in the still house?
The fire voice jars; there is no tune to the song
Of the thin wind at the door, and his nearest neighbour
Being three fields' breadth away, it more often seems
That bed is the shortest path to the friendlier morrow.

But he was not unhappy; there were souls to save;
Souls to be rescued from the encroaching wave
Of sin and evil. Morgan stirred the fire
And drove the shadows back into their corners.

THE MINISTER
I held a *seiat*, but no one came.
It was the wrong time, they said, there were the lambs,
And hay to be cut and peat to carry.
Winter was the time for that.
Winter is the time for easing the heart,
For swapping sins and recalling the days
Of summer when the blood was hot.

Ah, the blurred eye and the cold vein
Of age! 'Come home, come home. All is forgiven.'

I began a Bible class;
But no one came,
Only Mali, who was not right in the head.
She had a passion for me, and dreamed of the day . . .
I opened the Bible and expounded the Word
To the flies and spiders, as Francis preached to the birds.

NARRATOR
Over the moor the round sky
Was ripening, and the sun had spread
Its wings and now was heading south
Over the sea, where Morgan followed.
It was August, the holiday month
For ministers; they walked the smooth
Pavements of Aber and compared their lot
To the white accompaniment of the sea's laughter.

THE MINISTER
When I returned, strengthened, to the bare manse
That smelled of mould, someone had broken a window
During my absence and let a bird in.
I found it dead, starved, on the warm sill.
There is always the thin pane of glass set up between us
And our desires.
We stare and stare and stare, until the night comes
And the glass is superfluous.
I went to my cold bed saddened, but the wind in the tree
Outside soothed me with echoes of the sea.

NARRATOR
Harvest, harvest! The oats that were too weak
To hold their heads up had been cut down
And placed in stooks. There was no nonsense

Plaiting the last sheaf and wasting time
Throwing sickles. That was a fad of Prytherch
Of Nant Carfan; but the bugger was dead.
The men took the corn, the beautiful goddess,
By the long hair and threw her on the ground.

Below in the valleys they were thinking of Christmas;
The fields were all ploughed and the wheat in.
But Davies still hadn't made up his mind
Whom they should ask to the Thanksgiving.

The sea's tan had faded; the old pallor
Was back in Morgan's cheeks. In his long fight
With the bare moor, it was the moor that was winning.
The children came into Sunday School
Before he did, and put muck on his stool.
He stood for the whole lesson, pretending not to notice
The sounds in his desk: a mouse probably
Put there to frighten him. They loved their joke.
Say nothing, say nothing. Morgan was learning
To hold his tongue, the wisdom of the moor.
The pulpit is a kind of block-house
From which to fire the random shot
Of innuendo; but woe betide the man
Who leaves the pulpit for the individual
Assault. He spoke to Davies one day:

DAVIES

Adultery's a big word, Morgans: where's your proof?
You who never venture from under your roof
Once the night's come; the blinds all down
For fear of the moon's bum rubbing the window.
Take a word from me and keep your nose
In the Black Book, so it won't be tempted
To go sniffing where it's not wanted.
And leave us farmers to look to our own

Business, in case the milk goes sour
From your sharp talk before it's churned
To good butter, if you see what I mean.

NARRATOR

Did you say something?
Don't be too hard on them, there were people here
Before these and they were no better.
And there'll be people after may be, and they'll be
No better; it is the old earth's way
Of dealing with time's attrition.

Snow on the fields, snow on the heather;
The fox was abroad in the new moon
Barking. And if the snow thawed
And the roads cleared there was an election
Meeting in the vestry next the chapel.
Men came and spoke to them about Wales,
The land they lived in without knowing it,
The land that is reborn at such times.
They mentioned Henry Richard and S.R. – the great names;
And Keir Hardie; the names nobody knew.
It was quite exciting, but in the high marginal land
No names last longer than the wind
And the rain let them on the cold tombstone.
They stood outside afterwards and watched the cars
Of the speakers departing down the long road
To civilisation, and walked home
Arguing confusedly under the stars.

THE MINISTER

Winter was like that; a meeting, a foxhunt,
And the weekly journey to market to unlearn
The lesson of Sunday. The rain never kept them
From the packed town, though it kept them from chapel.

Drive on, farmer, to market
With your pigs and your lean cows
To the town, where the dealers are waiting
And the girl in the green blouse,
Fresh as a celandine from the spring meadows,
Builds like a fabulous tale
Tower upon tower on the counter
The brown and the golden ale.

NARRATOR

A year passed, once more Orion
Unsheathed his sword from its dark scabbard;
And Sirius followed, loud as a bird
Whistling to eastward his bright notes.
The stars are fixed, but the earth journeys
By strange migrations towards the cold
Frosts of autumn from the spring meadows.
And we who see them, where have we been
Since last their splendour inflamed our mind
With huge questions not to be borne?

Morgan was part of the place now; he was beginning
To look back as well as forwards:
Back to the green valleys, forward along the track
That dwindled to nothing in the vast moor.
But life still had its surprises. There was the day
They found old Llywarch dead under the wall
Of the grey sheep-fold, and the sheep all in a ring
Staring, staring at the stiff frame
And the pursed lips from which no whistle came.

THE MINISTER

It was my biggest funeral of all; the hills crawled
With black figures, drawn from remote farms
By death's magnet. 'So sudden. It might have been me.'

And there in the cheap coffin Llywarch was lying,
Taller than you thought, and women were trying
To read through their tears the brass plate.

It might have been Davies! Quickly I brushed
The black thought away; but it came back.
My voice deepened; the people were impressed.
Out in the cold graveyard we sang a hymn,
O fryniau Caersalem; and the Welsh hills looked on
Implacably. It was the old human cry.
But let me be fair, let me be fair.
It was not all like this, even the moor
Has moods of softness when the white hair
Of the bog cotton is a silk bed
For dreams to lie on. There was a day
When young Enid of Gors Fach
Pressed an egg into my hand
Smiling, and her father said:
'Take it, Morgans, to please the child.'
I never heard what they said after,
But went to my bed that night happy for once.
I looked from my top window and saw the moon,
Mellow with age, rising over the moor;
There was something in its bland expression
That softened the moor's harshness, stifled the questions
Struggling to my lips; I made a vow,
As other men in other years have done,
To-morrow would be different. I lay down
And slept quietly. But the morrow woke me
To the ancestral fury of the rain
Spitting and clawing at the pane.
I looked out on a grey world, grey with despair.

NARRATOR
The rhythm of the seasons: wind and rain,
Dryness and heat, and then the wind again,

Always the wind, and rain that is the sadness
We ascribe to nature, who can feel nothing.
The redwings leave, making way for the swallows;
The swallows depart, the redwings are back once more.
But man remains summer and winter through,
Rooting in vain within his dwindling acre.

THE MINISTER

I was the chapel pastor, the abrupt shadow
Staining the neutral fields, troubling the men
Who grew there with my glib, dutiful praise
Of a fool's world; a man ordained for ever
To pick his way along the grass-strewn wall
Dividing tact from truth.
                                        I knew it all,
Although I never pried, I knew it all.
I knew why Buddug was away from chapel.
I knew that Pritchard, the *Fron*, watered his milk.
I knew who put the ferret with the fowls
In Pugh's hen-house. I knew and pretended I didn't.
And they knew that I knew and pretended I didn't.
They listened to me preaching the unique gospel
Of love; but our eyes never met. And outside
The blood of God darkened the evening sky.

NARRATOR

Is there no passion in Wales? There is none
Except in the racked hearts of men like Morgan,
Condemned to wither and starve in the cramped cell
Of thought their fathers made them.
Protestantism – the adroit castrator
Of art; the bitter negation
Of song and dance and the heart's innocent joy –
You have botched our flesh and left us only the soul's
Terrible impotence in a warm world.

Need we go on? In spite of all
His courage Morgan could not avert
His failure, for he chose to fight
With that which yields to nothing human.
He never listened to the hills'
Music calling to the hushed
Music within; but let his mind
Fester with brooding on the sly
Infirmities of the hill people.
The pus conspired with the old
Infection lurking in his breast.

In the chapel acre there is a grave,
And grass contending with the stone
For mastery of the near horizon,
And on the stone words; but never mind them:
Their formal praise is a vain gesture
Against the moor's encroaching tide.
We will listen instead to the wind's text
Blown through the roof, or the thrush's song
In the thick bush that proved him wrong,
Wrong from the start, for nature's truth
Is primary and her changing seasons
Correct out of a vaster reason
The vague errors of the flesh.

from *Song at the Year's Turning* 1955

Children's Song

We live in our own world,
A world that is too small
For you to stoop and enter
Even on hands and knees,
The adult subterfuge.
And though you probe and pry
With analytic eye,
And eavesdrop all our talk
With an amused look,
You cannot find the centre
Where we dance, where we play,
Where life is still asleep
Under the closed flower,
Under the smooth shell
Of eggs in the cupped nest
That mock the faded blue
Of your remoter heaven.

The Village

Scarcely a street, too few houses
To merit the title; just a way between
The one tavern and the one shop
That leads nowhere and fails at the top
Of the short hill, eaten away
By long erosion of the green tide
Of grass creeping perpetually nearer
This last outpost of time past.

So little happens; the black dog
Cracking his fleas in the hot sun
Is history. Yet the girl who crosses
From door to door moves to a scale
Beyond the bland day's two dimensions.

Stay, then, village, for round you spins
On slow axis a world as vast
And meaningful as any poised
By great Plato's solitary mind.

Invasion on the Farm

I am Prytherch. Forgive me. I don't know
What you are talking about; your thoughts flow
Too swiftly for me; I cannot dawdle
Along their banks and fish in their quick stream
With crude fingers. I am alone, exposed
In my own fields with no place to run
From your sharp eyes. I, who a moment back
Paddled in the bright grass, the old farm
Warm as a sack about me, feel the cold
Winds of the world blowing. The patched gate
You left open will never be shut again.

January

The fox drags its wounded belly
Over the snow, the crimson seeds
Of blood burst with a mild explosion,
Soft as excrement, bold as roses.

Over the snow that feels no pity,
Whose white hands can give no healing,
The fox drags its wounded belly.

Pisces

Who said to the trout,
You shall die on Good Friday
To be food for a man
And his pretty lady?

It was I, said God,
Who formed the roses
In the delicate flesh
And the tooth that bruises.

The Return

Coming home was to that:
The white house in the cool grass
Membraned with shadow, the bright stretch
Of stream that was its looking-glass;

And smoke growing above the roof
To a tall tree among whose boughs
The first stars renewed their theme
Of time and death and a man's vows.

In a Country Church

To one kneeling down no word came,
Only the wind's song, saddening the lips
Of the grave saints, rigid in glass;
Or the dry whisper of unseen wings,
Bats not angels, in the high roof.

Was he balked by silence? He kneeled long,
And saw love in a dark crown
Of thorns blazing, and a winter tree
Golden with fruit of a man's body.

No Through Road

All in vain. I will cease now
My long absorption with the plough,
With the tame and the wild creatures
And man united with the earth.
I have failed after many seasons
To bring truth to birth,
And nature's simple equations
In the mind's precincts do not apply.

But where to turn? Earth endures
After the passing, necessary shame
Of winter, and the old lie
Of green places beckons me still
From the new world, ugly and evil,
That men pry for in truth's name.

from *Poetry for Supper* 1958

Evans

Evans? Yes, many a time
I came down his bare flight
Of stairs into the gaunt kitchen
With its wood fire, where crickets sang
Accompaniment to the black kettle's
Whine, and so into the cold
Dark to smother in the thick tide
Of night that drifted about the walls
Of his stark farm on the hill ridge.

It was not the dark filling my eyes
And mouth appalled me; not even the drip
Of rain like blood from the one tree
Weather-tortured. It was the dark
Silting the veins of that sick man
I left stranded upon the vast
And lonely shore of his bleak bed.

The Cat and the Sea

It is a matter of a black cat
On a bare cliff top in March
Whose eyes anticipate
The gorse petals;

The formal equation of
A domestic purr
With the cold interiors
Of the sea's mirror.

The Letter

And to be able to put at the end
Of the letter Athens, Florence – some name
That the spirit recalls from earlier journeys
Through the dark wood, seeking the path
To the bright mansions; cities and towns
Where the soul added depth to its stature.

And not to worry about the date,
The words being timeless, concerned with truth,
Beauty, love, misery even,
Which has its seasons in the long growth
From seed to flesh, flesh to spirit.

And laying aside the pen, dipped
Not in tears' volatile liquid
But in black ink of the heart's well,
To read again what the hand has written
To the many voices' quiet dictation.

The View from the Window

Like a painting it is set before one,
But less brittle, ageless; these colours
Are renewed daily with variations
Of light and distance that no painter
Achieves or suggests. Then there is movement,
Change, as slowly the cloud bruises
Are healed by sunlight, or snow caps
A black mood; but gold at evening
To cheer the heart. All through history
The great brush has not rested,
Nor the paint dried; yet what eye,
Looking coolly, or, as we now,
Through the tears' lenses, ever saw
This work and it was not finished?

Ap Huw's Testament

There are four verses to put down
For the four people in my life,
Father, mother, wife

And the one child. Let me begin
With her of the immaculate brow
My wife; she loves me. I know how.

My mother gave me the breast's milk
Generously, but grew mean after,
Envying me my detached laughter.

My father was a passionate man,
Wrecked after leaving the sea
In her love's shallows. He grieves in me.

What shall I say of my boy,
Tall, fair? He is young yet;
Keep his feet free of the world's net.

The Journey

And if you go up that way, you will meet with a man,
Leading a horse, whose eyes declare:
There is no God. Take no notice.
There will be other roads and other men
With the same creed, whose lips yet utter
Friendlier greeting, men who have learned
To pack a little of the sun's light
In their cold eyes, whose hands are waiting
For your hand. But do not linger.
A smile is payment; the road runs on
With many turnings towards the tall
Tree to which the believer is nailed.

Meet the Family

John One takes his place at the table,
He is the first part of the fable;
His eyes are dry as a dead leaf.
Look on him and learn grief.

John Two stands in the door
Dumb; you have seen that face before
Leaning out of the dark past,
Tortured in thought's bitter blast.

John Three is still outside
Drooling where the daylight died
On the wet stones; his hands are crossed
In mourning for a playmate lost.

John All and his lean wife,
Whose forced complicity gave life
To each loathed foetus, stare from the wall,
Dead not absent. The night falls.

The Cure

But what to do? Doctors in verse
Being scarce now, most poets
Are their own patients, compelled to treat
Themselves first, their complaint being
Peculiar always. Consider, you,
Whose rough hands manipulate
The fine bones of a sick culture,
What areas of that infirm body
Depend solely on a poet's cure.

Bread

Hunger was loneliness, betrayed
By the pitiless candour of the stars'
Talk, in an old byre he prayed

Not for food; to pray was to know
Waking from a dark dream to find
The white loaf on the white snow;

Not for warmth, warmth brought the rain's
Blurring of the essential point
Of ice probing his raw pain.

He prayed for love, love that would share
His rags' secret; rising he broke
Like sun crumbling the gold air

The live bread for the starved folk.

Farm Wife

Hers is the clean apron, good for fire
Or lamp to embroider, as we talk slowly
In the long kitchen, while the white dough
Turns to pastry in the great oven,
Sweetly and surely as hay making
In a June meadow; hers are the hands,
Humble with milking, but still now
In her wide lap as though they heard
A quiet music, hers being the voice
That coaxes time back to the shadows
In the room's corners. O, hers is all
This strong body, the safe island
Where men may come, sons and lovers,
Daring the cold seas of her eyes.

from *Tares* 1961

Walter Llywarch

I am, as you know, Walter Llywarch,
Born in Wales of approved parents,
Well goitred, round in the bum,
Sure prey of the slow virus
Bred in quarries of grey rain.

Born in autumn at the right time
For hearing stories from the cracked lips
Of old folk dreaming of summer,
I piled them on to the bare hearth
Of my own fancy to make a blaze
To warm myself, but achieved only
The smoke's acid that brings the smart
Of false tears into the eyes.

Months of fog, months of drizzle;
Thought wrapped in the grey cocoon
Of race, of place, awaiting the sun's
Coming, but when the sun came,
Touching the hills with a hot hand,
Wings were spread only to fly
Round and round in a cramped cage
Or beat in vain at the sky's window.

School in the week, on Sunday chapel:
Tales of a land fairer than this
Were not so tall, for others had proved it
Without the grave's passport, they sent
The fruit home for ourselves to taste.

Walter Llywarch – the words were a name
On a lost letter that never came
For one who waited in the long queue
Of life that wound through a Welsh valley.
I took instead, as others had done
Before, a wife from the back pews
In chapel, rather to share the rain
Of winter evenings, than to intrude
On her pale body; and yet we lay
For warmth together and laughed to hear
Each new child's cry of despair.

Anniversary

Nineteen years now
Under the same roof
Eating our bread,
Using the same air;
Sighing, if one sighs,
Meeting the other's
Words with a look
That thaws suspicion.

Nineteen years now
Sharing life's table,
And not to be first
To call the meal long
We balance it thoughtfully
On the tip of the tongue,
Careful to maintain
The strict palate.

Nineteen years now
Keeping simple house,
Opening the door
To friend and stranger;
Opening the womb
Softly to let enter
The one child
With his huge hunger.

Judgment Day

Yes, that's how I was,
I know that face,
That bony figure
Without grace
Of flesh or limb;
In health happy,
Careless of the claim
Of the world's sick
Or the world's poor;
In pain craven –
Lord, breathe once more
On that sad mirror,
Let me be lost
In mist for ever
Rather than own
Such bleak reflections,
Let me go back
On my two knees
Slowly to undo
The knot of life
That was tied there.

Hireling

Cars pass him by; he'll never own one.
Men won't believe in him for this.
Let them come into the hills
And meet him wandering a road,
Fenced with rain, as I have now;
The wind feathering his hair;
The sky's ruins, gutted with fire
Of the late sun, smouldering still.

Nothing is his, neither the land
Nor the land's flocks. Hired to live
On hills too lonely, sharing his hearth
With cats and hens, he has lost all
Property but the grey ice
Of a face splintered by life's stone.

R.S. THOMAS

Those Others

A gofid gwerin gyfan
Yn fy nghri fel taerni tân.
    Dewi Emrys

I have looked long at this land,
Trying to understand
My place in it – why,
With each fertile country
So free of its room,
This was the cramped womb
At last took me in
From the void of unbeing.

Hate takes a long time
To grow in, and mine
Has increased from birth;
Not for the brute earth
That is strong here and clean
And plain in its meaning
As none of the books are
That tell but of the war

Of heart with head, leaving
The wild birds to sing
The best songs; I find
This hate's for my own kind,
For men of the Welsh race
Who brood with dark face
Over their thin navel
To learn what to sell;

Yet not for them all either,
There are still those other
Castaways on a sea
Of grass, who call to me,
Clinging to their doomed farms;
Their hearts though rough are warm
And firm, and their slow wake
Through time bleeds for our sake.

Lore

Job Davies, eighty-five
Winters old, and still alive
After the slow poison
And treachery of the seasons.

Miserable? Kick my arse!
It needs more than the rain's hearse,
Wind-drawn, to pull me off
The great perch of my laugh.

What's living but courage?
Paunch full of hot porridge,
Nerves strengthened with tea,
Peat-black, dawn found me

Mowing where the grass grew,
Bearded with golden dew.
Rhythm of the long scythe
Kept this tall frame lithe.

What to do? Stay green.
Never mind the machine,
Whose fuel is human souls.
Live large, man, and dream small.

A Welsh Testament

All right, I was Welsh. Does it matter?
I spoke the tongue that was passed on
To me in the place I happened to be,
A place huddled between grey walls
Of cloud for at least half the year.
My word for heaven was not yours.
The word for hell had a sharp edge
Put on it by the hand of the wind
Honing, honing with a shrill sound
Day and night. Nothing that Glyn Dŵr
Knew was armour against the rain's
Missiles. What was descent from him?

Even God had a Welsh name:
We spoke to him in the old language;
He was to have a peculiar care
For the Welsh people. History showed us
He was too big to be nailed to the wall
Of a stone chapel, yet still we crammed him
Between the boards of a black book.

Yet men sought us despite this.
My high cheek-bones, my length of skull
Drew them as to a rare portrait
By a dead master. I saw them stare
From their long cars, as I passed knee-deep
In ewes and wethers. I saw them stand
By the thorn hedges, watching me string
The far flocks on a shrill whistle.
And always there was their eyes' strong
Pressure on me: You are Welsh, they said;
Speak to us so; keep your fields free
Of the smell of petrol, the loud roar

Of hot tractors; we must have peace
And quietness.
                        Is a museum
Peace? I asked. Am I the keeper
Of the heart's relics, blowing the dust
In my own eyes? I am a man;
I never wanted the drab rôle
Life assigned me, an actor playing
To the past's audience upon a stage
Of earth and stone; the absurd label
Of birth, of race hanging askew
About my shoulders. I was in prison
Until you came; your voice was a key
Turning in the enormous lock
Of hopelessness. Did the door open
To let me out or yourselves in?

Here

I am a man now.
Pass your hand over my brow,
You can feel the place where the brains grow.

I am like a tree,
From my top boughs I can see
The footprints that led up to me.

There is blood in my veins
That has run clear of the stain
Contracted in so many loins.

Why, then, are my hands red
With the blood of so many dead?
Is this where I was misled?

Why are my hands this way
That they will not do as I say?
Does no God hear when I pray?

I have nowhere to go.
The swift satellites show
The clock of my whole being is slow.

It is too late to start
For destinations not of the heart.
I must stay here with my hurt.

from *The Bread of Truth* 1963

The Survivors

I never told you this.
He told me about it often:
Seven days in an open boat – burned out,
No time to get food:
Biscuits and water and the unwanted sun,
With only the oars' wing-beats for motion,
Labouring heavily towards land
That existed on a remembered chart,
Never on the horizon
Seven miles from the boat's bow.

After two days song dried on their lips;
After four days speech.
On the fifth cracks began to appear
In the faces' masks; salt scorched them.
They began to think about death,
Each man to himself, feeding it
On what the rest could not conceal.
The sea was as empty as the sky,
A vast disc under a dome
Of the same vastness, perilously blue.

But on the sixth day towards evening
A bird passed. No one slept that night;
The boat had become an ear
Straining for the desired thunder
Of the wrecked waves. It was dawn when it came,
Ominous as the big guns
Of enemy shores. The men cheered it.
From the swell's rise one of them saw the ruins
Of all that sea, where a lean horseman
Rode towards them and with a rope
Galloped them up on to the curt sand.

Funeral

They stand about conversing
In dark clumps, less beautiful than trees.
What have they come here to mourn?
There was a death, yes; but death's brother,
Sin, is of more importance.
Shabbily the teeth gleam,
Sharpening themselves on reputations
That were firm once. On the cheap coffin
The earth falls more cleanly than tears.
What are these red faces for?
This incidence of pious catarrh
At the grave's edge? He has returned
Where he belongs; this is acknowledged
By all but the lonely few
Making amends for the heart's coldness
He had from them, grudging a little
The simple splendour of the wreath
Of words the church lays on him.

The Garden

It is a gesture against the wild,
The ungovernable sea of grass;
A place to remember love in,
To be lonely for a while;
To forget the voices of children
Calling from a locked room;
To substitute for the care
Of one querulous human
Hundreds of dumb needs.

It is the old kingdom of man.
Answering to their names,
Out of the soil the buds come,
The silent detonations
Of power wielded without sin.

R.S. THOMAS

The Untamed

My garden is the wild
  Sea of the grass. Her garden
Shelters between walls.
  The tide could break in;
  I should be sorry for this.

There is peace there of a kind,
  Though not the deep peace
Of wild places. Her care
  For green life has enabled
  The weak things to grow.

Despite my first love,
  I take sometimes her hand,
Following strait paths
  Between flowers, the nostril
  Clogged with their thick scent.

The old softness of lawns
  Persuading the slow foot
Leads to defection; the silence
  Holds with its gloved hand
  The wild hawk of the mind.

But not for long, windows,
  Opening in the trees
Call the mind back
  To its true eyrie; I stoop
  Here only in play.

Souillac: Le Sacrifice d'Abraham

And he grasps him by the hair
With innocent savagery.
And the son's face is calm;
There is trust there.

And the beast looks on.

This is what art could do,
Interpreting faith
With serene chisel.
The resistant stone
Is quiet as our breath,
And is accepted.

On the Farm

There was Dai Puw. He was no good.
They put him in the fields to dock swedes,
And took the knife from him, when he came home
At late evening with a grin
Like the slash of a knife on his face.

There was Llew Puw, and he was no good.
Every evening after the ploughing
With the big tractor he would sit in his chair,
And stare into the tangled fire garden,
Opening his slow lips like a snail.

There was Huw Puw, too. What shall I say?
I have heard him whistling in the hedges
On and on, as though winter
Would never again leave those fields,
And all the trees were deformed.

And lastly there was the girl:
Beauty under some spell of the beast.
Her pale face was the lantern
By which they read in life's dark book
The shrill sentence: God is love.

from *Pietà* 1966

Pietà

Always the same hills
Crowd the horizon,
Remote witnesses
Of the still scene.

And in the foreground
The tall Cross,
Sombre, untenanted,
Aches for the Body
That is back in the cradle
Of a maid's arms.

Ravens

It was the time of the election.
The ravens loitered above the hill
In slow circles; they had all air
To themselves. No eyes were lifted
From the streets, no ears heard
Them exulting, recalling their long
History, presidents of the battles
Of flesh, the sly connoisseurs
Of carrion; desultory flags
Of darkness, saddening the sky
At Catraeth and further back,
When two, who should have been friends,
Contended in the innocent light
For the woman in her downpour of hair.

The Moor

It was like a church to me.
I entered it on soft foot,
Breath held like a cap in the hand.
It was quiet.
What God was there made himself felt,
Not listened to, in clean colours
That brought a moistening of the eye,
In movement of the wind over grass.

There were no prayers said. But stillness
Of the heart's passions – that was praise
Enough; and the mind's cession
Of its kingdom. I walked on,
Simple and poor, while the air crumbled
And broke on me generously as bread.

There

They are those that life happens to.
They didn't ask to be born
In those bleak farmsteads, but neither
Did they ask not. Life took the seed
And broadcast it upon the poor,
Rush-stricken soil, an experiment
In patience.
                    What is a man's
Price? For promises of a break
In the clouds; for harvests that are not all
Wasted; for one animal born
Healthy, where seven have died,
He will kneel down and give thanks
In a chapel whose stones are wrenched
From the moorland.
                                I have watched them bent
For hours over their trade,
Speechless, and have held my tongue
From its question. It was not my part
To show them, like a meddler from the town,
Their picture, nor the audiences
That look at them in pity or pride.

The Belfry

I have seen it standing up grey,
Gaunt, as though no sunlight
Could ever thaw out the music
Of its great bell; terrible
In its own way, for religion
Is like that. There are times
When a black frost is upon
One's whole being, and the heart
In its bone belfry hangs and is dumb.

But who is to know? Always,
Even in winter in the cold
Of a stone church, on his knees
Someone is praying, whose prayers fall
Steadily through the hard spell
Of weather that is between God
And himself. Perhaps they are warm rain
That brings the sun and afterwards flowers
On the raw graves and throbbing of bells.

Aside

Take heart, Prytherch.
Over you the planets stand,
And have seen more ills than yours.
This canker was in the bone
Before man bent to his image
In the pool's glass. Violence has been
And will be again. Between better
And worse is no bad place

For a labourer, whose lot is to seem
Stationary in traffic so fast.
Turn aside, I said; do not turn back.
There is no forward and no back
In the fields, only the year's two
Solstices, and patience between.

The Face

When I close my eyes, I can see it,
That bare hill with the man ploughing,
Corrugating that brown roof
Under a hard sky. Under him is the farm,
Anchored in its grass harbour;
And below that the valley
Sheltering its few folk,
With the school and the inn and the church,
The beginning, middle and end
Of their slow journey above ground.

He is never absent, but like a slave
Answers to the mind's bidding,
Endlessly ploughing, as though autumn
Were the one season he knew.
Sometimes he pauses to look down
To the grey farmhouse, but no signals
Cheer him; there is no applause
For his long wrestling with the angel
Of no name. I can see his eye
That expects nothing, that has the rain's
Colourlessness. His hands are broken
But not his spirit. He is like bark
Weathering on the tree of his kind.

He will go on; that much is certain.
Beneath him tenancies of the fields
Will change; machinery turn
All to noise. But on the walls
Of the mind's gallery that face
With the hills framing it will hang
Unglorified, but stern like the soil.

from *Not That He Brought Flowers* 1968

Careers

Fifty-two years,
most of them taken in
growing or in the
illusion of it – what does the mem-ory
number as one's
property? The broken elbow?
the lost toy? The pain has
vanished, but the soft flesh
that suffered it is mine still.

There is a house with
a face mooning at the glass
of windows. Those eyes – I look
at not with them, but something of
their melancholy I
begin to lay claim to as my own.

A boy in school:
his lessons are
my lessons, his
punishments I learn to deserve.
I stand up in him,
tall as I am
now, but without per-spective.

Distant objects
are too distant, yet will arrive
soon. How his words
muddle me; how my deeds
betray him. That is not
our intention; but where I should
be one with him, I am one now
with another. Before I had time
to complete myself, I let her share
in the building. This that I am
now – too many
labourers. What is mine is
not mine only: her love, her
child wait for my slow
signature. Son, from the mirror
you hold to me I turn
to recriminate. That likeness
you are at work upon – it hurts.

St Julian and the Leper

Though all ran from him, he did not
Run, but awaited
Him with his arms
Out, his ears stopped
To his bell, his alarmed
Crying. He lay down
With him there, sharing his sores'
Stench, the quarantine
Of his soul; contaminating
Himself with a kiss,
With the love that
Our science has disinfected.

Concession

Not that he brought flowers
Except for the eyes' blue,
Perishable ones, or that his hands,
Famed for kindness were put then
To such usage; but rather that, going
Through flowers later, she yet could feel
These he spared perhaps for my sake.

Shrine at Cape Clear

She is more white than the sea's
Purest spray, and colder
To touch. She is nourished
By salt winds, and the prayers
Of the drowned break on her. She smiles
At the stone angels, who have turned
From the sea's truth to worship
The mystery of her dumb child.

The bay brings her the tribute
Of its silences. The ocean has left
An offering of the small flowers
Of its springs; but the men read,
Beyond the harbour on the horizon,
The fury of its obituaries.

The Fisherman

A simple man,
He liked the crease on the water
His cast made, but had no pity
For the broken backbone
Of water or fish.

One of his pleasures, thirsty,
Was to ask a drink
At the hot farms;
Leaving with a casual thank you,
As though they owed it him.

I could have told of the living water
That springs pure.
He would have smiled then,
Dancing his speckled fly in the shallows,
Not understanding.

Sailors' Hospital

It was warm
Inside, but there was
Pain there. I came out
Into the cold wind
Of April. There were birds
In the brambles' old,
Jagged iron, with one striking
Its small song. To the west,
Rising from the grey
Water, leaning one
On another were the town's
Houses. Who first began
That refuse: time's waste
Growing at the edge
Of the clean sea? Some sailor,
Fetching up on the
Shingle before wind
Or current, made it his
Harbour, hung up his clothes
In the sunlight; found women
To breed from – those sick men
His descendants. Every day
Regularly the tide
Visits them with its salt
Comfort; their wounds are shrill
In the rigging of the
Tall ships.
            With clenched thoughts,
That not even the sky's
Daffodil could persuade
To open, I turned back
To the nurses in their tugging
At him, as he drifted

Away on the current
Of his breath, further and further,
Out of hail of our love.

Reservoirs

There are places in Wales I don't go:
Reservoirs that are the subconscious
Of a people, troubled far down
With gravestones, chapels, villages even;
The serenity of their expression
Revolts me, it is a pose
For strangers, a watercolour's appeal
To the mass, instead of the poem's
Harsher conditions. There are the hills,
Too; gardens gone under the scum
Of the forests; and the smashed faces
Of the farms with the stone trickle
Of their tears down the hills' side.

Where can I go, then, from the smell
Of decay, from the putrefying of a dead
Nation? I have walked the shore
For an hour and seen the English
Scavenging among the remains
Of our culture, covering the sand
Like the tide and, with the roughness
Of the tide, elbowing our language
Into the grave that we have dug for it.

Kneeling

Moments of great calm,
Kneeling before an altar
Of wood in a stone church
In summer, waiting for the God
To speak; the air a staircase
For silence; the sun's light
Ringing me, as though I acted
A great rôle. And the audiences
Still; all that close throng
Of spirits waiting, as I,
For the message.
                    Prompt me, God;
But not yet. When I speak,
Though it be you who speak
Through me, something is lost.
The meaning is in the waiting.

Tenancies

This is pain's landscape.
A savage agriculture is practised
Here; every farm has its
Grandfather or grandmother, gnarled hands
On the cheque-book, a long, slow
Pull on the placenta about the neck.
Old lips monopolise the talk
When a friend calls. The children listen
From the kitchen; the children march
With angry patience against the dawn.
They are waiting for someone to die
Whose name is as bitter as the soil
They handle. In clear pools
In the furrows they watch themselves grow old
To the terrible accompaniment of the song
Of the blackbird, that promises them love.

The Small Window

In Wales there are jewels
To gather, but with the eye
Only. A hill lights up
Suddenly; a field trembles
With colour and goes out
In its turn; in one day
You can witness the extent
Of the spectrum and grow rich

With looking. Have a care;
This wealth is for the few
And chosen. Those who crowd
A small window dirty it
With their breathing, though sublime
And inexhaustible the view.

from *H'm* 1972

Once

God looked at space and I appeared,
Rubbing my eyes at what I saw.
The earth smoked, no birds sang:
There were no footprints on the beaches
Of the hot sea, no creatures in it
God spoke. I hid myself in the side
Of the mountain.
                           As though born again
I stepped out into the cool dew,
Trying to remember the fire sermon,
Astonished at the mingled chorus
Of weeds and flowers. In the brown bark
Of the Trees I saw the many faces
Of life, forms hungry for birth,
Mouthing at me. I held my way
To the light, inspecting my shadow
Boldly; and in the late morning
You, rising towards me out of the depths
Of myself. I took your hand,
Remembering you, and together,
Confederates of the natural day,
We went forth to meet the Machine.

Petition

And I standing in the shade
Have seen it a thousand times
Happen: first theft, then murder;
Rape; the rueful acts
Of the blind hand. I have said
New prayers, or said the old
In a new way. Seeking the poem
In the pain, I have learned
Silence is best, paying for it
With my conscience. I am eyes
Merely, witnessing virtue's
Defeat; seeing the young born
Fair, knowing the cancer
Awaits them. One thing I have asked
Of the disposer of the issues
Of life: that truth should defer
To beauty. It was not granted.

R. S. THOMAS

Invitation

And one voice says: Come
Back to the rain and manure
Of Siloh, to the small talk,
Of the wind, and the chapel's

Temptation; to the pale,
Sickly half-smile of
The daughter of the village
Grocer. The other says: Come

To the streets, where the pound
Sings and the doors open
To its music, with life
Like an express train running

To time. And I stay
Here, listening to them, blowing
On the small soul in my
Keeping with such breath as I have.

Song

I choose white, but with
Red on it, like the snow
In winter with its few
Holly berries and the one

Robin, that is a fire
To warm by and like Christ
Comes to us in his weakness,
But with a sharp song.

Acting

Being unwise enough to have married her
I never knew when she was not acting.
'I love you' she would say; I heard the audiences
Sigh. 'I hate you'; I could never be sure
They were still there. She was lovely. I
Was only the looking-glass she made up in.
I husbanded the rippling meadow
Of her body. Their eyes grazed nightly upon it.

Alone now on the brittle platform
Of herself she is playing her last rôle.
It is perfect. Never in all her career
Was she so good. And yet the curtain
Has fallen. My charmer, come out from behind
It to take the applause. Look, I am clapping too.

Pavane

Convergences
Of the spirit! What
Century, love? I,
Too; you remember –
Brescia? This sunlight reminds
Of the brocade. I dined
Long. And now the music
Of darkness in your eyes
Sounds. But Brescia,
And the spreading foliage
Of smoke! With Yeats' birds
Grown hoarse.
    Artificer
Of the years, is this
Your answer? The long dream
Unwound; we followed
Through time to the tryst
With ourselves. But wheels roll
Between and the shadow
Of the plane falls. The
Victim remains
Nameless on the tall
Steps. Master, I
Do not wish, I do not wish
To continue.

R.S. THOMAS

The Hearth

In front of the fire
With you, the folk song
Of the wind in the chimney and the sparks'
Embroidery of the soot – eternity
Is here in this small room,
In intervals that our love
Widens; and outside
Us is time and the victims
Of time, travellers
To a new Bethlehem, statesmen
And scientists with their hands full
Of the gifts that destroy.

84

The Island

And God said, I will build a church here
And cause this people to worship me,
And afflict them with poverty and sickness
In return for centuries of hard work
And patience. And its walls shall be hard as
Their hearts, and its windows let in the light
Grudgingly, as their minds do, and the priest's words be drowned
By the wind's caterwauling. All this I will do,

Said God, and watch the bitterness in their eyes
Grow, and their lips suppurate with
Their prayers. And their women shall bring forth
On my altars, and I will choose the best
Of them to be thrown back into the sea.

And that was only on one island.

The River

And the cobbled water
Of the stream with the trout's indelible
Shadows that winter
Has not erased — I walk it
Again under a clean
Sky with the fish, speckled like thrushes,
Silently singing among the weed's
Branches.

        I bring the heart
Not the mind to the interpretation
Of their music, letting the stream
Comb me, feeling it fresh
In my veins, revisiting the sources
That are as near now
As on the morning I set out from them.

All Right

I look. You look
Away. No colour,
No ruffling of the brow's
Surface betrays
Your feeling. As though I
Were not here; as
Though you were your own
Mirror, you arrange yourself
For the play. My eyes'
Adjectives; the way that
I scan you; the
Conjunction the flesh
Needs – all these
Are as nothing
To you. Serene, cool,
Motionless, no statue
Could show less
The impression of
My regard. Madam, I
Grant the artistry
Of your part. Let us
Consider it, then,
A finished performance.

Soliloquy

And God thought: Pray away,
Creatures; I'm going to destroy
It. The mistake's mine,
If you like. I have blundered
Before; the glaciers erased
My error.
        I saw them go
Further than you – palaces,
Missiles. My privacy
Was invaded; then the flaw
Took over; they allied themselves
With the dust. Winds blew away
Their pasture. Their bones signalled
From the desert to me
In vain.
        After the dust, fire;
The earth burned. I have forgotten
How long, but the fierce writing
Seduced me. I blew with my cool
Breath; the vapour condensed
In the hollows. The sun was torn
From my side. Out of the waters
You came, as subtle
As water, with your mineral
Poetry and promises
Of obedience. I listened to you
Too long. Within the churches
You built me you genuflected
To the machine. Where will it
Take you from the invisible
Viruses, the personnel
Of the darkness that do my will?

That Day

Stopped the car, asked a man the way
To some place; he rested on it
Smiling, an impression of charm
As of ripe fields; talking to us
He held a reflection of sky
In his brushed eyes. We lost interest
In the way, seeing him old
And content, feeling the sun's warmth
In his voice, watching the swallows
Above him – thirty years back
To this summer. Knowing him gone,
We wander the same flower-bordered road,
Seeing the harvest ripped from the land,
Deafened by the planes' orchestra;
Unable to direct the lost travellers
Or convince them this is a good place to be.

H'm

and one said
speak to us of love
and the preacher opened
his mouth and the word God
fell out so they tried
again speak to us
of God then but the preacher
was silent reaching
his arms out but the little
children the ones with
big bellies and bow
legs that were like
a razor shell
were too weak to come

The Kingdom

It's a long way off but inside it
There are quite different things going on:
Festivals at which the poor man
Is king and the consumptive is
Healed; mirrors in which the blind look
At themselves and love looks at them
Back; and industry is for mending
The bent bones and the minds fractured
By life. It's a long way off, but to get
There takes no time and admission
Is free, if you will purge yourself
Of desire, and present yourself with
Your need only and the simple offering
Of your faith, green as a leaf.

Other

It was perfect. He could do
Nothing about it. Its waters
Were as clear as his own eye. The grass
Was his breath. The mystery
Of the dark earth was what went on
In himself. He loved and
Hated it with a parent's
Conceit, admiring his own
Work, resenting its
Independence. There were trysts
In the greenwood at which
He was not welcome. Youths and girls,
Fondling the pages of
A strange book, awakened
His envy. The mind achieved
What the heart could not. He began planning
The destruction of the long peace
Of the place. The machine appeared
In the distance, singing to itself
Of money. Its song was the web
They were caught in, men and women
Together. The villages were as flies
To be sucked empty.
                    God secreted
A tear. Enough, enough,
He commanded, but the machine
Looked at him and went on singing.

The Fair

The idiot goes round and around
With his brother in a bumping car
At the fair. The famous idiot
Smile hangs over the car's edge,
Illuminating nothing. This is mankind
Being taken for a ride by a rich
Relation. The responses are fixed:
Bump, smile; bump, smile. And the current

Is generated by the smooth flow
Of the shillings. This is an orchestra
Of steel with the constant percussion
Of laughter. But where he should be laughing
Too, his features are split open, and look!
Out of the cracks come warm, human tears.

from *Young and Old* 1972

Madam

And if you ask her
she has no name;
but her eyes say:
Water is cold.

She is three years old
and willing to kiss;
but her lips say:
Apples are sour.

from *Laboratories of the Spirit* 1975

The Hand

It was a hand. God looked at it
and looked away. There was a coldness
about his heart, as though the hand
clasped it. As at the end
of a dark tunnel, he saw cities
the hand would build, engines
that it would raze them with. His sight
dimmed. Tempted to undo the joints
of the fingers, he picked it up.
But the hand wrestled with him. 'Tell
me your name,' it cried, 'and I will write it
in bright gold. Are there not deeds
to be done, children to make, poems
to be written? The world
is without meaning, awaiting
my coming.' But God, feeling the nails
in his side, the unnerving warmth
of the contact, fought on in
silence. This was the long war with himself
always foreseen, the question not
to be answered. What is the hand
for? The immaculate conception
preceding the delivery

of the first tool? 'I let you go,'
he said, 'but without blessing.
Messenger to the mixed things
of your making, tell them I am.'

Out There

It is another country.
There is no speech there such
as we know; even the colours
                          are different.
When the residents use their eyes,
it is not shapes they see but the distance
between them. If they go,
it is not in a traveller's
usual direction, but sideways and
out through the mirror of a refracted
timescale. If you met them early,
you would recognize them by an absence
of shadow. Your problems
                          are in their past;
those they are about to solve
are what you are incapable
of conceiving. In experiments
in outbreeding, under the growing microscope
of the mind, they are isolating
the human virus and burning it
up in the fierceness of their detachment.

Amen

It was all arranged:
the virgin with child, the birth
in Bethlehem, the arid journey uphill
to Jerusalem. The prophets foretold
it, the scriptures conditioned him
to accept it. Judas went to his work
with his sour kiss; what else
could he do?
                    A wise old age,
the honours awarded for lasting,
are not for a saviour. He had
to be killed; salvation acquired
by an increased guilt. The tree,
with its roots in the mind's dark,
was divinely planted, the original fork
in existence. There is no meaning in life,
unless men can be found to reject
love. God needs his martyrdom.
The mild eyes stare from the Cross
in perverse triumph. What does he care
that the people's offerings are so small?

That Place

I served on a dozen committees;
talked hard, said little, shared the applause
at the end. Picking over
the remains later, we agreed power
was not ours, launched our invective
at others, the anonymous wielders
of such. Life became small, grey,
the smell of interiors. Occasions
on which a clean air entered our nostrils
off swept seas were instances
we sought to recapture. One particular
time after a harsh morning
of rain, the clouds lifted, the wind
fell; there was a resurrection
of nature, and we there to emerge
with it into the anointed
air. I wanted to say to you: 'We
will remember this.' But tenses
were out of place on that green
island, ringed with the rain's
bow, that we had found and would spend
the rest of our lives looking for.

Good Friday

It was quiet. What had the sentry
to cry, but that it was the ninth hour
and all was not well? The darkness
began to lift, but it was not the mind

was illumined. The carpenter
had done his work well to sustain
the carpenter's burden; the Cross an example
of the power of art to transcend timber.

The Chapel

A little aside from the main road,
becalmed in a last-century greyness,
there is the chapel, ugly, without the appeal
to the tourist to stop his car
and visit it. The traffic goes by,
and the river goes by, and quick shadows
of clouds, too, and the chapel settles
a little deeper into the grass.

But here once on an evening like this,
in the darkness that was about
his hearers, a preacher caught fire
and burned steadily before them
with a strange light, so that they saw
the splendour of the barren mountains
about them and sang their amens
fiercely, narrow but saved
in a way that men are not now.

The Casualty

I had forgotten
   the old quest for truth
      I was here for. Other cares

held me: urgencies
   of the body; a girl
      beckoned; money

had never appeared
   so ethereal; it was God's blood
      circulating in the veins

of creation; I partook
   of it like Communion, lost
      myself on my way

home, with the varying voices
   on call. Moving backward
      into a receding

future, I lost the use
   of perspective, borrowing poetry
      to buy my children

their prose. The past was a poor
   king, rendering his crown down
      for the historian. Every day

I went on with that
   metallic warfare in which
      the one casualty is love.

Probing

No one would know you had lived,
but for my discovery
of the anonymous undulation
of your grave, like the early swelling
of the belly of a woman
who is with child. And if I entered
it now, I would find your bones
huddled together, but without
flesh, their ruined architecture
a reproach, the skull luminous
but not with thought.

                  Would it help us to learn
what you were called in your forgotten
language? Are not our jaws
frail for the sustaining of the consonants'
weight? Yet they were balanced
on tongues like ours, echoed
in the ears' passages, in intervals when
the volcano was silent. How
tenderly did the woman handle
them, as she leaned her haired body
to yours? Where are the instruments
of your music, the pipe of hazel, the
bull's horn, the interpreters
of your loneliness on this
ferocious planet?

                  We are domesticating
it slowly; but at times it rises
against us, so that we see again
the primeval shadows you built
your fire amongst. We are cleverer
than you; our nightmares

are intellectual. But we never awaken
from the compulsiveness of the mind's
stare into the lenses' furious interiors.

The Flower

I asked for riches.
You gave me the earth, the sea,
                    the immensity
of the broad sky. I looked at them
and learned I must withdraw
      to possess them. I gave my eyes
      and my ears, and dwelt
in a soundless darkness
                 in the shadow
      of your regard.
              The soul
      grew in me, filling me
with its fragrance.
             Men came
to me from the four
      winds to hear me speak
      of the unseen flower by which
I sat, whose roots were not
in the soil, nor its petals the colour
of the wide sea; that was
      its own species with its own
      sky over it, shot
with the rainbow of your coming and going.

The Moon in Lleyn

The last quarter of the moon
of Jesus gives way
to the dark; the serpent
digests the egg. Here
on my knees in this stone
church, that is full only
of the silent congregation
of shadows and the sea's
sound, it is easy to believe
Yeats was right. Just as though
choirs had not sung, shells
have swallowed them; the tide laps
at the Bible; the bell fetches
no people to the brittle miracle
of the bread. The sand is waiting
for the running back of the grains
in the wall into its blond
glass. Religion is over, and
what will emerge from the body
of the new moon, no one
can say.

        But a voice sounds
in my ear: Why so fast,
mortal? These very seas
are baptized. The parish
has a saint's name time cannot
unfrock. In cities that
have outgrown their promise people
are becoming pilgrims
again, if not to this place,
then to the recreation of it
in their own spirits. You must remain
kneeling. Even as this moon

making its way through the earth's
cumbersome shadow, prayer, too,
has its phases.

Hill Christmas

They came over the snow to the bread's
purer snow, fumbled it in their huge
hands, put their lips to it
like beasts, stared into the dark chalice
where the wine shone, felt it sharp
on their tongue, shivered as at a sin
remembered, and heard love cry
momentarily in their hearts' manger.

They rose and went back to their poor
holdings, naked in the bleak light
of December. Their horizon contracted
to the one small, stone-riddled field
with its tree, where the weather was nailing
the appalled body that had not asked to be born.

The Combat

You have no name.
We have wrestled with you all
day, and now night approaches,
the darkness from which we emerged
seeking; and anonymous
you withdraw, leaving us nursing
our bruises, our dislocations.

For the failure of language
there is no redress. The physicists
tell us your size, the chemists
the ingredients of your
thinking. But who you are
does not appear, nor why
on the innocent marches
of vocabulary you should choose
to engage us, belabouring us
with your silence. We die, we die
with the knowledge that your resistance
is endless at the frontier of the great poem.

Somewhere

Something to bring back to show
you have been there: a lock of God's
hair, stolen from him while he was
asleep; a photograph of the garden
of the spirit. As has been said,
the point of travelling is not
to arrive, but to return home
laden with pollen you shall work up
into the honey the mind feeds on.

What are our lives but harbours
we are continually setting out
from, airports at which we touch
down and remain in too briefly
to recognize what it is they remind
us of? And always in one
another we seek the proof
of experiences it would be worth dying for.

Surely there is a shirt of fire
this one wore, that is hung up now
like some rare fleece in the hall of heroes?
Surely these husbands and wives
have dipped their marriages in a fast
spring? Surely there exists somewhere,
as the justification for our looking for it,
the one light that can cast such shadows?

Alive

It is alive. It is you,
God. Looking out I can see
no death. The earth moves, the
sea moves, the wind goes
on its exuberant
journeys. Many creatures
reflect you, the flowers
your colour, the tides the precision
of your calculations. There
is nothing too ample
for you to overflow, nothing
so small that your workmanship
is not revealed. I listen
and it is you speaking.
I find the place where you lay
warm. At night, if I waken,
there are the sleepless conurbations
of the stars. The darkness
is the deepening shadow
of your presence; the silence a
process in the metabolism
of the being of love.

Marriage

I look up; you pass.
I have to reconcile your
existence and the meaning of it
with what I read: kings and queens
and their battles
for power. You have your battle,
too. I ask myself: Have
I been on your side? Lovelier
a dead queen than a live
wife? History worships
the fact but cannot remain
neutral. Because there are no kings
worthy of you; because poets
better than I are not here
to describe you; because time
is always too short, you must go by
now without mention, as unknown
to the future as to
the past, with one man's
eyes resting on you
in the interval of his concern.

Montrose

It is said that he went gaily to that scaffold,
dressed magnificently as a bridegroom,
his lace lying on him like white frost
in the windless morning of his courage.

His red blood was the water of life,
changed to wine at the wedding banquet;
the bride Scotland, the spirit dependent on
such for the consummation of her marriage.

The Bright Field

I have seen the sun break through
to illuminate a small field
for a while, and gone my way
and forgotten it. But that was the pearl
of great price, the one field that had
the treasure in it. I realize now
that I must give all that I have
to possess it. Life is not hurrying

on to a receding future, nor hankering after
an imagined past. It is the turning
aside like Moses to the miracle
of the lit bush, to a brightness
that seemed as transitory as your youth
once, but is the eternity that awaits you.

Llananno

I often call there.
There are no poems in it
for me. But as a gesture
of independence of the speeding
traffic I am a part
of, I stop the car,
turn down the narrow path
to the river, and enter
the church with its clear reflection
beside it.
        There are few services
now; the screen has nothing
to hide. Face to face
with no intermediary
between me and God, and only the water's
quiet insistence on a time
older than man, I keep my eyes
open and am not dazzled,
so delicately does the light enter
my soul from the serene presence
that waits for me till I come next.

Sea-Watching

Grey waters, vast
    as an area of prayer
that one enters. Daily
    over a period of years
I have let the eye rest on them.
Was I waiting for something?
                          Nothing
but that continuous waving
    that is without meaning
occurred.
    Ah, but a rare bird is
rare. It is when one is not looking,
at times one is not there
                    that it comes.
You must wear your eyes out,
as others their knees.
    I became the hermit
of the rocks, habited with the wind
and the mist. There were days,
so beautiful the emptiness
it might have filled,
            its absence
was as its presence; not to be told
any more, so single my mind
after its long fast,
          my watching from praying.

from *The Way of It* 1977

Barn Owl

1

Mostly it is a pale
face hovering in the afterdraught
of the spirit, making both ends meet
on a scream. It is the breath
of the churchyard, the forming
of white frost in a believer,
when he would pray; it is soft
feathers camouflaging a machine.

It repeats itself year
after year in its offspring,
the staring pupils it teaches
its music to, that is the voice
of God in the darkness cursing himself
fiercely for his lack of love.

2

and there the owl happens
like white frost as
cruel and as silent
and the time on its
blank face is not
now so the dead
have nothing to go

by and are fast
or slow but never punctual
as the alarm is
over their bleached bones
of its night-strangled cry.

The Way of It

With her fingers she turns paint
into flowers, with her body
flowers into a remembrance
of herself. She is at work
always, mending the garment
of our marriage, foraging
like a bird for something
for us to eat. If there are thorns
in my life, it is she who
will press her breast to them and sing.

Her words, when she would scold,
are too sharp. She is busy
after for hours rubbing smiles
into the wounds. I saw her,
when young, and spread the panoply
of my feathers instinctively
to engage her. She was not deceived,
but accepted me as a girl
will under a thin moon
in love's absence as someone
she could build a home with
for her imagined child.

from *Frequencies* 1978

The Porch

Do you want to know his name?
It is forgotten. Would you learn
what he was like? He was like
anyone else, a man with ears
and eyes. Be it sufficient
that in a church porch on an evening
in winter, the moon rising, the frost
sharp, he was driven
to his knees and for no reason
he knew. The cold came at him;
his breath was carved angularly
as the tombstones; an owl screamed.

He had no power to pray.
His back turned on the interior
he looked out on a universe
that was without knowledge
of him and kept his place
there for an hour on that lean
threshold, neither outside nor in.

The Woman

So beautiful – God himself quailed
at her approach: the long body curved
like the horizon. Why had he made
her so? How would it be, she said,
leaning towards him, if, instead of
quarrelling over it, we divided it
between us? You can have all the credit
for its invention, if you will leave the ordering
of it to me. He looked into her
eyes and saw far down the bones
of the generations that would navigate
by those great stars, but the pull of it
was too much. Yes, he thought, give me their minds'
tribute, and what they do with their bodies
is not my concern. He put his hand in his side
and drew out the thorn for the letting
of the ordained blood and touched her with
it. Go, he said. They shall come to you for ever
with their desire, and you shall bleed for them in return.

Night Sky

What they are saying is
that there is life there, too;
that the universe is the size it is
to enable us to catch up.

They have gone on from the human;
that shining is a reflection
of their intelligence. Godhead
is the colonisation by mind

of untenanted space. It is its own
light, a statement beyond language
of conceptual truth. Every night
is a rinsing myself of the darkness

that is in my veins. I let the stars inject me
with fire, silent as it is far,
but certain in its cauterising
of my despair. I am a slow

traveller, but there is more than time
to arrive. Resting in the intervals
of my breathing, I pick up the signals
relayed to me from a periphery I comprehend.

The Small Country

Did I confuse the categories?
Was I blind?
Was I afraid of hubris
in identifying this land
with the kingdom? Those stories
about the far journeys, when it was here
at my door; the object
of my contempt that became
the toad with the jewel in its head!
Was a population so small
enough to be called, too many
to be chosen? I called it
an old man, ignoring the April
message proclaiming: Behold,
I make all things new.

The dinosaurs have gone their way
into the dark. The time-span
of their human counterparts
is shortened; everything
on this shrinking planet favours the survival
of the small people, whose horizons
are large only because they are content to look at them
from their own hills.
                    I grow old,
bending to enter the promised
land that was here all the time,
happy to eat the bread that was baked
in the poets' oven, breaking my speech
from the perennial tree
of my people and holding it in my blind hand.

Pre-Cambrian

Here I think of the centuries,
six million of them, they say.
Yesterday a fine rain fell;
today the warmth has brought out the crowds.
After Christ, what? The molecules
are without redemption. My shadow
sunning itself on this stone
remembers the lava. Zeus looked down
on a brave world, but there was
no love there; the architecture
of their temples was less permanent
than these waves. Plato, Aristotle,
all those who furrowed the calmness
of their foreheads are responsible
for the bomb. I am charmed here
by the serenity of the reflections
in the sea's mirror. It is a window
as well. What I need
now is a faith to enable me to out-stare
the grinning faces of the inmates of its asylum,
the failed experiments God put away.

Adjustments

Never known as anything
but an absence, I dare not name him
as God. Yet the adjustments
are made. There is an unseen
power, whose sphere is the cell
and the electron. We never catch
him at work, but can only say,
coming suddenly upon an amendment,
that here he has been. To demolish
a mountain you move it stone by stone
like the Japanese. To make a new coat
of an old, you add to it gradually
thread by thread, so such change
as occurs is more difficult to detect.

Patiently with invisible structures
he builds, and as patiently
we must pray, surrendering the ordering
of the ingredients to a wisdom that
is beyond our own. We must change the mood
to the passive. Let the deaf men
be helped; in the silence that has come
upon them, let some influence
work so those closed porches
be opened once more. Let the bomb
swerve. Let the raised knife of the murderer
be somehow deflected. There are no
laws there other than the limits of
our understanding. Remembering rock
penetrated by the grass-blade, corrected
by water, we must ask rather

for the transformation of the will
to evil, for more loving
mutations, for the better ventilating
of the atmosphere of the closed mind.

The Empty Church

They laid this stone trap
for him, enticing him with candles,
as though he would come like some huge moth
out of the darkness to beat there.
Ah, he had burned himself
before in the human flame
and escaped, leaving the reason
torn. He will not come any more

to our lure. Why, then, do I kneel still
striking my prayers on a stone
heart? Is it in hope one
of them will ignite yet and throw
on its illumined walls the shadow
of someone greater than I can understand?

In Great Waters

You are there also
at the foot of the precipice
of water that was too steep
for the drowned: their breath broke
and they fell. You have made an altar
out of the deck of the lost
trawler whose spars
are your cross. The sand crumbles
like bread; the wine is
the light quietly lying
in its own chalice. There is
a sacrament there more beauty
than terror whose ministrant
you are and the aisles are full
of the sea shapes coming to its celebration.

Roger Bacon

He had strange dreams
    that were real
in which he saw God
    showing him an aperture
      of the horizon wherein
were flasks and test-tubes.
    And the rainbow
ended there not in a pot
    of gold, but in colours
that, dissected, had the ingredients of
    the death ray.

Faces at the window
    of his mind
had the false understanding
of flowers, but their eyes pointed
    like arrows to
    an imprisoning cell.
                   Yet
he dreamed on in curves
    and equations
with the smell of saltpetre
in his nostrils, and saw the hole
    in God's side that is the wound
      of knowledge and
thrust his hand in it and believed.

Emerging

Well, I said, better to wait
for him on some peninsula
of the spirit. Surely for one
with patience he will happen by
once in a while. It was the heart
spoke. The mind, sceptical as always
of the anthropomorphisms
of the fancy, knew he must be put together
like a poem or a composition
in music, that what he conforms to
is art. A promontory is a bare
place; no God leans down
out of the air to take the hand
extended to him. The generations have
watched there
in vain. We are beginning to see
now it is matter is the scaffolding
of spirit; that the poem emerges
from morphemes and phonemes; that
as form in sculpture is the prisoner
of the hard rock, so in everyday life
it is the plain facts and natural happenings
that conceal God and reveal him to us
little by little under the mind's tooling.

The White Tiger

It was beautiful as God
must be beautiful; glacial
eyes that had looked on
violence and come to terms

with it; a body too huge
and majestic for the cage in which
it had been put; up
and down in the shadow

of its own bulk it went,
lifting, as it turned,
the crumpled flower of its face
to look into my own

face without seeing me. It
was the colour of the moonlight
on snow and as quiet
as moonlight, but breathing

as you can imagine that
God breathes within the confines
of our definition of him, agonising
over immensities that will not return.

R. S. THOMAS

The Film of God

Sound, too? The recorder
that picks up everything picked
up nothing but the natural
background. What language
does the god speak? And the camera's
lens, as sensitive to
an absence as to a presence,
saw what? What is the colour
of his thought?

        It was blank, then,
the screen, as far as he
was concerned? It was a bare
landscape and harsh, and geological
its time. But the rock was
bright, the illuminated manuscript
of the lichen. And a shadow,
as we watched, fell, as though
of an unseen writer bending over
his work.

        It was not cloud
because it was not cold,
and dark only from the candlepower
behind it. And we waited
for it to move, silently
as the spool turned, waited
for the figure that cast it
to come into view for us to
identify it, and it
didn't and we are still waiting.

The Absence

It is this great absence
that is like a presence, that compels
me to address it without hope
of a reply. It is a room I enter

from which someone has just
gone, the vestibule for the arrival
of one who has not yet come.
I modernise the anachronism

of my language, but he is no more here
than before. Genes and molecules
have no more power to call
him up than the incense of the Hebrews

at their altars. My equations fail
as my words do. What resource have I
other than the emptiness without him of my whole
being, a vacuum he may not abhor?

from *Between Here and Now* 1981

Pilgrimages

There is an island there is no going
to but in a small boat the way
the saints went, travelling the gallery
of the frightened faces of
the long-drowned, munching the gravel
of its beaches. So I have gone
up the salt lane to the building
with the stone altar and the candles
gone out, and kneeled and lifted
my eyes to the furious gargoyle
of the owl that is like a god
gone small and resentful. There
is no body in the stained window
of the sky now. Am I too late?
Were they too late also, those
first pilgrims? He is such a fast
God, always before us and
leaving as we arrive.

                  There are those here
not given to prayer, whose office
is the blank sea that they say daily.
What they listen to is not
hymns but the slow chemistry of the soil
that turns saints' bones to dust,
dust to an irritant of the nostril.

There is no time on this island.
The swinging pendulum of the tide
has no clock; the events
are dateless. These people are not
late or soon; they are just
here with only the one question
to ask, which life answers
by being in them. It is I
who ask. Was the pilgrimage
I made to come to my own
self, to learn that in times
like these and for one like me
God will never be plain and
out there, but dark rather and
inexplicable, as though he were in here?

Directions

In this desert of language
   we find ourselves in,
with the sign-post with the word 'God'
   worn away
             and the distance . . . ?

Pity the simpleton
   with his mouth open crying:
          How far is it to God?

And the wiseacre says: Where you were,
friend.
   You know that smile
               glossy
as the machine that thinks it has outpaced
   belief?
        I am one of those
who sees from the arms opened
        to embrace the future
the shadow of the Cross fall
   on the smoothest of surfaces
        causing me to stumble.

Waiting

Yeats said that. Young
I delighted in it:
there was time enough.

Fingers burned, heart
seared, a bad taste
in the mouth, I read him

again, but without trust
any more. What counsel
has the pen's rhetoric

to impart? Break mirrors, stare
ghosts in the face, try
walking without crutches

at the grave's edge? Now
in the small hours
of belief the one eloquence

to master is that
of the bowed head, the bent
knee, waiting, as at the end

of a hard winter
for one flower to open
on the mind's tree of thorns.

Pluperfect

It was because there was nothing to do
that I did it; because silence was golden
I broke it. There was a vacuum
I found myself in, full of echoes
of dead languages. Where to turn
when there are no corners? In curved
space I kept on arriving
at my departures. I left no stones
unraised, but always wings
were tardy to start. In ante-rooms
of the spirit I suffered the anaesthetic
of time and came to with my hurt
unmended. Where are you? I
shouted, growing old in
the interval between here and now.

Fair Day

They come in from the fields
with the dew and the buttercup dust
on their boots. It was not they
nor their ancestors crucified
Christ. They look up at what
the town has done to him,
hanging his body in stone on a stone
cross, as though to commemorate
the bringing of the divine beast
to bay and disabling him.

He is hung up high, but higher
are the cranes and scaffolding
of the future. And they stand by,
men from the past, whose rôle
is to assist in the destruction
of the past, bringing their own beasts
in to offer their blood up
on a shoddier altar.
          The town
is malignant. It grows, and what
it feeds on is what these men call
their home. Is there praise
here? There is the noise of those
buying and selling and mortgaging
their conscience, while the stone
eyes look down tearlessly. There
is not even anger in them any more.

Seventieth Birthday

Made of tissue and H_2O,
and activated by cells
firing — Ah, heart, the legend
of your person! Did I invent
it, and is it in being still?

In the competition with other
women your victory is assured.
It is time, as Yeats said, is
the caterpillar in the cheek's rose,
the untiring witherer of your petals.

You are drifting away from
me on the whitening current of your hair.
I lean far out from the bone's bough,
knowing the hand I extend
can save nothing of you but your love.

Mediterranean

The water is the same;
it is the reflections are different.
Virgil looked in this
mirror. You would not think so.

The lights' jewellery sticks in the throat
of the fish; open
them, you will find a debased
coinage to pay your taxes.

The cicadas sing
on. Looking for them among
the ilex is like trying to translate
a poem into another language.

Beacons

Whose address was the corridors
of Europe, waiting for the summons
to be interrogated on their lack of guilt.

Their flesh was dough for the hot
ovens. Some of them rose
to the occasion. The nerves of some

were instruments on which the guards fingered
obscene music. Were there prayers
said? Did a god hear? Time heard

them, anticipating their requital.
Their wrong is an echo defying
acoustical law, increasing not fading.

Evil's crumbling anonymity
is at an end now. We recognise
it by the eternal phosphorous

of their bones, and make our way on
by that same light to the birth
of an innocence that is curled up in the will.

Flowers

But behind the flower
is that other flower
which is ageless, the idea
of the flower, the one
we smell when we imagine
it, that as often
as it is picked blossoms
again, that has the perfection
of all flowers, the purity
without the fragility.
                              Was it
a part of the plan
for humanity to have
flowers about it? They are many
and beautiful, with faces
that are a reminder of those
of our own children, though they come painlessly
from the bulb's womb. We trouble
them as we go by, so they hang
their heads at our unreal
progress.
              If flowers had minds,
would they not think they were the colour
eternity is, a window that gives
on a still view the hurrying
people must come to and stare at and pass by?

R. S. THOMAS

Minor

Nietzsche had a word
for it. History discredits
his language. Ours
more quietly rusts

in autumnal libraries
of the spirit. Scolded
for small faults, we see
how violence in others

is secretly respected.
Do we amble pacifically
towards our extinction? The answers
from over the water

are blood-red. I wonder,
seeing the rock
split by green grass
as efficiently

as the atom, is this
the centre from which
nature will watch out
human folly, until

it is time to call back
to the small field civilisation
began in the small
people the giants deposed?

Forest Dwellers

Men who have hardly uncurled
from their posture in the
womb. Naked. Heads bowed, not
in prayer, but in contemplation
of the earth they came from,
that suckled them on the brown
milk that builds bone not brain.

Who called them forth to walk
in the green light, their thoughts
on darkness? Their women,
who are not Madonnas, have babes
at the breast with the wise,
time-ridden faces of the Christ
child in a painting by a Florentine

master. The warriors prepare poison
with love's care for the Sebastians
of their arrows. They have no
God, but follow the contradictions
of a ritual that says
life must die that life
may go on. They wear flowers in their hair.

from *Later Poems* 1983

Threshold

I emerge from the mind's
cave into the worse darkness
outside, where things pass and
the Lord is in none of them.

I have heard the still, small voice
and it was that of the bacteria
demolishing my cosmos. I
have lingered too long on

this threshold, but where can I go?
To look back is to lose the soul
I was leading upward towards
the light. To look forward? Ah,

what balance is needed at
the edges of such an abyss.
I am alone on the surface
of a turning planet. What

to do but, like Michelangelo's
Adam, put my hand
out into unknown space,
hoping for the reciprocating touch?

Covenanters

JESUS

He wore no hat, but he produced, say
from up his sleeve, an answer
to their question about
the next life. It is here,
he said, tapping his forehead
as one would to indicate
an idiot. The crowd frowned

and took up stones
to punish his adultery
with the truth. But he, stooping
to write on the ground, looked
sideways at them, as they withdrew
each to the glass-house of his own mind.

MARY

Model of models;
virgin smile over
the ageless babe,

my portrait is in
the world's galleries:
motherhood without

a husband; chastity
my complexion. Cradle
of flesh for one

not born of the flesh,
Alas, you painters
of a half-truth, the

poets excel you.
They looked in under
my lids and saw

as through a stained glass
window the hill
the infant must climb,

the crookedness of
the kiss he appended
to his loving epistle.

JOSEPH
I knew what I knew.
She denied it.
I went with her
on the long journey.
My seed was my own
seed, was the star
that the wise men
followed. Their gifts were no good
to us. I taught him
the true trade: to go
with the grain.
        He left me
for a new master
who put him to the fashioning
of a cross for himself.

LAZARUS
That imperious summons! Spring's
restlessness among dry
leaves. He stands at the grave's
entrance and rubs death from his eyes,
while thought's fountain recommences
its play, watering the waste ground

over again for the germination
of the blood's seed, where roses should blow.

JUDAS ISCARIOT
picked flowers stole birds' eggs
like the rest was his mother's
fondling passed under the tree
he would hang from without
realising looked through the branches
saw only the cloud face
of God and the sky mirroring
the water he was brought up by

was a shrewd youth with a talent
for sums became treasurer
to the disciples was genuinely
hurt by a certain extravagance
in the Master went out of his own
free will to do that which he had to do.

PAUL
Wrong question, Paul. Who am I,
Lord? is what you should have asked.
And the answer, surely, somebody
who it is easy for us to kick against.
There were some matters you were dead right
about. For instance, I like you
on love. But marriage – I would have thought
too many had been burned in that fire
for your contrast to hold.
                           Still, you are the mountain
the teaching of the carpenter of Nazareth
congealed into. The theologians
have walked round you for centuries
and none of them scaled you. Your letters remain
unanswered, but survive the recipients

of them. And we, pottering among the foot-hills
of their logic, find ourselves staring
across deep crevices at conclusions at which
the living Jesus would not willingly have arrived.

Gradual

I have come to the borders
of the understanding. Instruct
me, God, whether to press
onward or to draw back.

To say I am a child
is a pretence at humility
that is unworthy of me.
Rather am I at one with those

minds, all of whose instruments
are beside the point of
their sharpness. I need a technique
other than that of physics

for registering the ubiquity
of your presence. A myriad prayers
are addressed to you in a thousand
languages and you decode

them all. Liberty for you
is freedom from our too human
senses, yet we die
when they nod. Call your horizons

in. Suffer the domestication
for a moment of the ferocities
you inhabit, a garden for us to refine
our ignorance in under the boughs of love.

Strays

Of all the women of the fields –
    full skirt, small waist –
the scarecrow is the best dressed.

She has an air about her
    which more than makes up
for her loss of face.

There is nothing between us.
    If I take her arm
there is nowhere to go.

We are alone and strollers
    of a fine day with
under us the earth's fathoms waiting.

History

It appears before us,
   wringing its dry hands,
quoting from Nietzsche's book,
   from Schopenhauer.

Sing us, we say,
   more sunlit occasions;
the child by the still pool
   multiplying reflections.

It remains unconsoled
   in its dust-storm of tears,
remembering the Crusades,
   the tortures, the purges.

But time passes by;
   it commits adultery
with it to father the cause
   of its continued weeping.

Questions

Prepare yourself for the message.
You are prepared?
                    Silence.
Silence is the message.
The message is . . . Wait.
Are you sure? An echo?
An echo of an echo?
                    Sound.
Was it always there
            with us failing
to hear it?
            What was the shell doing
on the shore? An ear endlessly
            drinking?
            What? Sound? Silence?
Which came first?
            Listen.
I'll tell you a story
as it was told me by the teller
            of stories.
Where did he hear it?
By listening? To silence? To sound?
          To an echo? To an echo
            of an echo?
            Wait.

The Bush

I know that bush,
Moses; there are many of them
in Wales in the autumn, braziers
where the imagination
warms itself. I have put off
pride and, knowing the ground
holy, lingered to wonder
how it is that I do not burn
and yet am consumed.

And in this country
of failure, the rain
falling out of a black
cloud in gold pieces there
are none to gather,
I have thought often
of the fountain of my people
that played beautifully here
once in the sun's light
like a tree undressing.

R.S. THOMAS

Suddenly

Suddenly after long silence
he has become voluble.
He addresses me from a myriad
directions with the fluency
of water, the articulateness
of green leaves; and in the genes,
too, the components
of my existence. The rock,
so long speechless, is the library
of his poetry. He sings to me
in the chain-saw, writes
with the surgeon's hand
on the skin's parchment messages
of healing. The weather
is his mind's turbine
driving the earth's bulk round
and around on its remedial
journey. I have no need
to despair; as at
some second Pentecost
of a Gentile, I listen to the things
round me: weeds, stones, instruments,
the machine itself, all
speaking to me in the vernacular
of the purposes of One who is.

Arrival

Not conscious
   that you have been seeking
     suddenly
   you come upon it

the village in the Welsh hills
     dust free
   with no road out
but the one you came in by.

   A bird chimes
   from a green tree
the hour that is no hour
   you know. The river dawdles
to hold a mirror for you
where you may see yourself
   as you are, a traveller
     with the moon's halo
   above him, who has arrived
   after long journeying where he
     began, catching this
   one truth by surprise
that there is everything to look forward to.

Remembering David Jones

Because you had been in the dark wood
and heard doom's nightingales sing,
men listened to you when you told
them how death is many but life
one. The shell's trumpet sounded
over the fallen, but there was no
resurrection. You learned your lettering
from bones, the propped capitals which described
how once they were human beings.

Men march because they are alive,
and their quest is the Grail, garrisoned
by the old furies so it is blood
wets their lips. Europe gave you
your words, but your hand practised
an earlier language, weaving time's branches
together to form the thicket the soldier
is caught in, who is love's sacrifice
to itself, with the virgin's smile poised
like a knife over it as over her first born.

The Moment

Is the night dark? His interiors
are darker, more perilous
to enter. Are there whispers
abroad? They are the communing

with himself our destiny
is to be outside of, listeners
at our breath's window. Is there
an ingredient in him of unlove?

It is the moment in the mind's
garden he resigns himself
to his own will to conceive the tree
of manhood we have reared against him.

R. S. THOMAS

Carol

What is Christmas without
snow? We need it
as bread of a cold
climate, ermine to trim

our sins with, a brief
sleeve for charity's
scarecrow to wear its heart
on, bold as a robin.

from *Ingrowing Thoughts* 1985

Prayer

Baudelaire's grave
not too far
from the tree of science.
Mine, too,
since I sought and failed
to steal from it,
somewhere within sight
of the tree of poetry
that is eternity wearing
the green leaves of time.

from *Experimenting with an Amen* 1986

Formula

And for the soul
in its bone tent, refrigerating
under the nuclear winter,
no epitaph prepared

in our benumbed language
other than the equation
hanging half-mast like the after-
birth of thought: $E = mc^2$.

Cones

Simple in your designs,
infinite in your variations
upon them: the leaf's veins,
the shell's helix, the stars themselves
gyring down to a point
in the mind; the mind also
from that same point spiralling
outward to take in space.

Heartening that in our journeys
through time we come round not
to the same place, but recognise it
from a distance. It is the dream
we remember, that makes us say:
'We have been here before.' In
truth we are as far from it
as one side of the cone
from the other, and in between
are the false starts, the failures,
the ruins from which we climbed,
not to look down, but to feel your glance
resting on us at the next angle
of the gyre.
            God, it is not your reflections
we seek, wonderful as they are
in the live fibre; it is the possibility
of your presence at the cone's
point towards which we soar
in hope to arrive at the still
centre, where love operates
on all those frequencies
that are set up by the spinning
of two minds, the one on the other.

Coming

To be crucified
again? To be made friends
with for his jeans and beard?
Gods are not put to death

any more. Their lot now
is with the ignored.
I think he still comes
stealthily as of old,

invisible as a mutation,
an echo of what the light
said, when nobody
attended; an impression

of eyes, quicker than
to be caught looking, but taken
on trust like flowers in the
dark country towards which we go.

He and She

When he came in, she was there.
When she looked at him
he smiled. There were lights
in time's wave breaking
on an eternal shore.

Seated at table,
no need for the fracture
of the room's silence; noiselessly
they conversed. Thoughts mingling
were lit up, gold
particles in the mind's stream.

Were there currents between them?
Why when he thought darkly
would the nerves play
at her lips' brim? What was the heart's depth?
There were fathoms in her,
too, and sometimes he crossed
them and landed and was not repulsed.

R. S. THOMAS

The Fly

And the fly said: 'Nothing
to do. May as well
alight here.' No luck;
no poison. So man walked
immune down avenues
of vast promise, seeking
perfection. The fly
had it; filled in the time
flying, embroidering space
with the invisible meshwork
of flight's thread; spun rainbows
from light's spectrum. Man
worked more purposely
at his plans: immortality,
truth; killing the things would not
be killed, like time, love,
the one human, the other
one of the fly's ilk.
                    What
is perfection? Anonymity's
patent? A frame fitted
for effortless success
in conveying viruses
to the curved nostril?
                    I will not
be here long, but have seen
(among people) distorted
bodies, haloed with love,
shedding a radiance
where flies hung smaller
than the dust they say
man came from and to which,
I say, he will not return.

Gift

Some ask the world
　　and are diminished
in the receiving
　　of it. You gave me

only this small pool
　　that the more I drink
from, the more overflows
　　me with sourceless light.

Destinations

Travelling towards the light
we were waylaid by darkness;
a formless company detained us,
saying everything, meaning nothing.

'It is a conspiracy,' I said,
'of great age in revolt
against reason, against all
that would be ethereal in us.'

We looked at one another.
Was it the silence of agreement,
or the vacuum between two minds
not in contact? There is an ingredient

in thought that is its own
hindrance. Had we come all that way
to detect it? The voices combined
urging us to put our trust

in the bone's wisdom. 'Remember'
they charged us, 'the future
for which you are bound is where
you began.' Was there a counter

command? I listened as to
a tideless sea on a remote
star, and knew our direction
was elsewhere; to the light, yes,

but not such as minerals
deploy, to the brightness over
an interior horizon, which is science
transfiguring itself in love's mirror.

Harvest End
(From the Welsh of Caledfryn)

The seasons fly;
the flowers wither;
the leaves lie
on the ground. Listen
to the sad song
of the reapers: 'Ripe
corn', as over the sea
the birds go.

Suddenly the year
ends. The wind rages;
everything in its path
breaks. Dire weather;
in front of a stick
fire, fetched from
the forest, firm and infirm
cower within doors.

The longest of lives
too soon slips by.
Careers fold and with
them good looks fade.
Spring's bloom is spent,
summer is done, too.
With a rush we come
to winter in the grave.

The Wood

A wood.
A man entered;
thought he knew the way
through. The old furies
attended. Did he emerge
in his right mind? The same
man? How many years
passed? Aeons? What is
the right mind? What does
'same' mean? No change of clothes
for the furies? Fast
as they are cut down
the trees grow, new
handles for axes.
There is a rumour from the heart
of the wood: brow
furrowed, mind
smooth, somebody huddles
in wide contemplation – Buddha,
Plato, Blake, Jung –
the name changes, identity
remains, pure being waiting
to be come at. Is it the self
that he mislaid? Is it why
he entered, ignoring
the warning of the labyrinth
without end? How many times
over must he begin again?

Sarn Rhiw

So we know
she must have said something
to him – What language,
life? Oh, what language?

Thousands of years later
I inhabit a house
whose stone is the language
of its builders. Here

by the sea they said little.
But their message to the future
was: Build well. In the fire
of an evening I catch faces

staring at me. In April,
when light quickens and clouds
thin, boneless presences
flit through my room.

Will they inherit me
one day? What certainties
have I to hand on
like the punctuality

with which, at the moon's
rising, the bay breaks
into a smile as though meaning
were not the difficulty at all?

Ritual

Not international
renown, but international
vocabulary, the macaronics
of time: μοῖρα, desiderium,
brad, la vida
breve, despair – I am the bone
on which all have beaten out
their message to the mind
that would soar. Faithful
in translation, its ploy was to evade
my resources. It saw
me dance through the Middle
Ages, and wrote its poetry
with quilled pen. What
so rich as the language
to which the priests
buried me? They have exchanged
their vestments for white coats,
working away in their bookless
laboratories, ministrants
in that ritual beyond words
which is the Last Sacrament of the species.

Calling

The telephone is the fruit
of the tree of the knowledge
of good and evil. We may call
everyone up on it but God.

To do that is to declare
that he is far off. Dialling
zero is nothing other
than the negation of his presence.

So many times I have raised
the receiver, listening to
that smooth sound that is technology's
purring; and the temptation

has come to experiment
with the code which would put
me through to the divine
snarl at the perimeter of such tameness.

Countering

Then there is the clock's
commentary, the continuing
prose that is the under-current
of all poetry. We listen
to it as, on a desert island,
men do to the subdued
music of their blood in a shell.

Then take my hand that is
of the bone the island
is made of, and looking at
me say what time it is
on love's face, for we have
no business here other than
to disprove certainties the clock knows.

The Window

Say he is any man
anywhere set before the shop window
of life, full of comestibles
and jewels; to put out his hand
is to come up against
glass; to break it is
to injure himself.
                        Shall he turn
poet and acquire them
in the imagination, gospeller
and extol himself for his abstention
from them?
                        What if he is not
called? I would put the manufacturers
there. Let them see the eyes
staring in, be splashed with the blood
of the shop-breakers; let them live
on the poet's diet, on the pocket-money
of the priest.
                        I see the blinds
going down in Europe, over the
whole world: the rich with everything to
sell, the poor with nothing to buy it with.

Retirement

I have crawled out at last
far as I dare on to a bough
of country that is suspended
between sky and sea.

From what was I escaping?
There is a rare peace here,
though the aeroplanes buzz me,
reminders of that abyss,

deeper than sea or sky, civilisation
could fall into. Strangers.
advance, inching their way
out, so that the branch bends

further away from the scent
of the cloud blossom. Must
I console myself
with reflections? There are

times even the mirror
is misted as by one breathing
over my shoulder. Clinging
to my position, witnessing

the seasonal migrations,
I must try to content
myself with the perception
that love and truth have

no wings, but are resident
like me here, practising
their sub-song quietly in the face
of the bitterest of winters.

Looking Glass

There is a game I play
with a mirror, approaching
it when I am not there,
as though to take by surprise

the self that is my familiar. It
is in vain. Like one eternally
in ambush, fast or slow
as I may raise my head, it raises

its own, catching me in the act,
disarming me by acquaintance,
looking full into my face as often
as I try looking at it askance.

Bequest

Wanting peace we were misled
by a dead nation's counsel
to prepare for war. Thinking love
would survive an instruction
in violence we took ourselves back
to a dark school, terrified
ourselves with our own propaganda.

As Germans their nostrils
with bad smells, we inoculated
ourselves with the poison factories
in our meadows. Our scientists
had white coats, vestments
these of a clandestine ritual.

Somewhere from under an old
dustbin lid you will have emerged
for the re-assembling of the species.
We have left you nothing
but the consequences of our refusal
to sit down by the still pool
in the mind, waiting for the unknown
visitant's quickening of its surface.

A Thicket in Lleyn

I was no tree walking.
I was still. They ignored me,
the birds, the migrants
on their way south. They re-leafed
the trees, budding them
with their notes. They filtered through
the boughs like sunlight,
looked at me from three feet
off, their eyes blackberry bright,
not seeing me, not detaching me
from the withies, where I was
caged and they free.
              They would have perched
on me, had I had nourishment
in my fissures. As it was,
they netted me in their shadows,
brushed me with sound, feathering the arrows
of their own bows, and were gone,
leaving me to reflect on the answer
to a question I had not asked.
'A repetition in time of the eternal
I AM.' Say it. Don't be shy.
Escape from your mortal cage
in thought. Your migrations will never
be over. Between two truths
there is only the mind to fly with.
Navigate by such stars as are not
leaves falling from life's
deciduous tree, but spray from the fountain
of the imagination, endlessly
replenishing itself out of its own waters.

Nativity

The moon is born
and a child is born,
lying among white clothes
as the moon among clouds.

They both shine, but
the light from the one
is abroad in the universe
as among broken glass.

Jerusalem

A city – its name
keeps it intact. Don't
touch it. Let the muezzin's
cry, the blood call

of the Christian, the wind
from sources desiccated
as the spirit drift over
its scorched walls. Time

devourer of its children
chokes here on the fact
it is in high places love
condescends to be put to death.

Moorland

It is beautiful and still;
      the air rarefied
as the interior of a cathedral

expecting a presence. It is where, also,
      the harrier occurs,
materialising from nothing, snow-

soft, but with claws of fire,
      quartering the bare earth
for the prey that escapes it;

hovering over the incipient
      scream, here a moment, then
not here, like my belief in God.

A Life

Lived long; much fear, less
courage. Bottom in love's school
of his class; time's reasons
too far back to be known.
Good on his knees, yielding,
vertical, to petty temptations.
A mouth thoughts escaped
from unfledged. Where two
were company, he the unwanted
third. A Narcissus tortured
by the whisperers behind
the mirror. Visionary only
in his perception of an horizon
beyond the horizon. Doubtful
of God, too pusillanimous
to deny him. Saving his face
in verse from the humiliations prose
inflicted on him. One of life's
conscientious objectors, conceding
nothing to the propaganda of death
but a compulsion to volunteer.

Folk Tale

Prayers like gravel
    flung at the sky's
window, hoping to attract
        the loved one's
attention. But without
    visible plaits to let
down for the believer
        to climb up,
to what purpose open
    that far casement?
        I would
have refrained long since
    but that peering once
through my locked fingers
I thought that I detected
    the movement of a curtain.

Message

A message from God
delivered by a bird
at my window, offering friendship.
Listen. Such language!
Who said God was without
speech? Every word an injection
to make me smile. Meet me,
it says, to-morrow here
at the same time and you will remember
how wonderful to-day
was: no pain, no worry;
irrelevant the mystery, if
unsolved. I gave you the X-ray
eye for you to use not
to prospect, but to discover
the un-malignancy of love's
growth. You were a patient, too,
anaesthetised on truth's table
with life operating on you
with a green scalpel. Meet me, I say,
to-morrow and I will sing it for you
all over again, when you have come to.

Andante

Masters, you who would initiate
me in discourse, apostrophising
the deity: O Thou, to Whom . . .
out of date three hundred
years. The atoms translate
into their own terms, burnishing
the dust, converting it
to a presence, a movement of light
on the room's wall, a smile quickening
and going out as the clouds
canter. Inhabitants of a flower
they fix that gaze on us
which is without focus, but compels
the attention, mesmerising us until
we are adrift on its scent's timelessness.
The huskiness of an emotion!
Can molecules feel? There is the long sigh
from the shore, the wave clearing
its throat to address us, requiring
no answer than the due
we give these things that share
the world with us, that compose
the world: an ever-renewed
symphony to be listened to
admiringly, even as we perform
it on whatever instruments
the generations put into our hands.

A Country

It is nowhere,
    and I am familiar
with it as one is
with a song.
        I know its background,
           the terraces
of cloud that are the hanging gardens
        of the imagination.
No sun
    rises there, so there is no sun
to set. It is the mind
suffuses it with a light
    that is without
        shadows.
           Invisible fountains
play, though their skirts
are of silk.
        And who lives there,
you ask, who walks
its unmetalled highways?
        It is a people
who pay their taxes
        in poetry; who repair broken
names; who wear the past
as a button-hole at their children's
        marriage with what is to be.

Reply

Do the wheels praise,
    humming to themselves
as they proceed in unnecessary
    directions? Do the molecules
bow down? Before what cradle
    do the travellers from afar,
strontium and plutonium, hold out
    their thin gifts? What
is missing from the choruses
    of bolts and rivets, as they prepare
for the working of their expensive
    miracle high in the clerestories
of blind space? What anthem have our computers
    to insert into the vacuum caused
by the break in transmission
    of the song upon Patmos?

Cures

'We sat under a tree
at the season when elms
put forth their leaves. It was then
Guillemette Benet said to me:
"My poor friend, my poor friend,
the soul is nothing
but blood." '*

        So the deposition
at Foix. Inquisitor,
what would you have the soul
be to escape the rigour
of your laundering? Your Christ
died for you; for whom
would you have these die?
No answer. He has withdrawn
iron-faced into the silence
from which history resurrects
everything but our reasons.

Meanwhile a few leagues
to the west, like a suppuration
of grace, the soiled fountain
plays, where the scientists gather
bacteria. Their claims are refuted
by the virgin smile on the face
of the water. Holy Church
has become wise, recognising
the anaemic soul is no substitute
for the bone's need.
        And the mind,
then, weary of the pilgrimages

* From *Montaillou* by Emmanuel le Roy Ladurie, translated by Barbara Bray.

to its horizons – is there no spring of thought
adjacent to it, where it can be
dipped, so that emerging but
once in ten thousand times,
freed of its crutches, is sufficient
testimony to the presence in it
of a power other than its own?

from *Welsh Airs* 1987

Drowning

They were irreplaceable and forgettable,
inhabitants of the parish and speakers
of the Welsh tongue. I looked on and
there was one less and one less and one less.

They were not of the soil, but contributed
to it in dying, a manure not
to be referred to as such, but from which
poetry is grown and legends and green tales.

Their immortality was what they hoped for
by being kind. Their smiles were such as,
exercised so often, became perennial
as flowers, blossoming where they had been cut down.

I ministered uneasily among them until
what had been gaps in the straggling hedgerow
of the nation widened to reveal the emptiness
that was inside, where echoes haunted and thin ghosts.

A rare place, but one identifiable
with other places where on as deep a sea
men have clung to the last spars of their language
and gone down with it, unremembered but uncomplaining.

Fugue for Ann Griffiths

In which period
    do you get lost?
The roads lead
    under a twentieth century
sky to the peace
    of the nineteenth. There it is,
as she left it,
    too small to be chrysalis
of that clenched soul.
    Under the eaves the martins
continue her singing.
    Down this path she set off
for the earlier dancing
    of the body; but under the myrtle
the Bridegroom was waiting
    for her on her way home.

To put it differently
yet the same, listen,
friend:
        A nineteenth century
                            calm;
that is, a countryside
    not fenced in
by cables and pylons,
but open to thought to blow in
    from as near as may be
to the truth.
            There were evenings
she would break it. See her
    at the dance, round
and round, hand
    in hand, weaving

invisible threads. When
you are young . . . But
    there was One
with his eye on her;
    she saw him stand
under the branches.
           History insists
on a marriage, but the husband was as cuckolded
as Joseph.
      Listen again:

To the knocker at the door:
'Miss Thomas has gone dancing.'

To the caller in time:
'The mistress is sitting the dance

out with God at her side.'
To the traveller up learning's

slope: 'She is ahead of you on her knees.
She who had decomposed

is composed again in her hymns.
The dust settles on the Welsh language,

but is blown away in great gusts
week by week in chapel after chapel.'

Is there a scholarship that grows
naturally as the lichen? How
did she, a daughter of the land, come
by her learning? You have seen
her face, figure-head of a ship
outward bound? But she was not
alone; a trinity of persons
saw to it she kept on course
like one apprenticed since early
days to the difficulty of navigation
in rough seas. She described her turbulence

to her confessor, who was the more
astonished at the fathoms
of anguish over which she had
attained to the calmness of her harbours.

There are other pilgrimages
    to make beside Jerusalem, Rome;
beside the one into the no-man's-
    land beyond the microscope's carry.

If you came in winter,
    you would find the tree
with your belief still crucified
    upon it, that for her at all

times was in blossom, the resurrection
    of one that had come seminally
down to raise the deciduous human
    body to the condition of his body.

Hostilities were other peoples'.
Though a prisoner of the Lord
she was taken without fighting.

That was in the peace before
the wars that were to end
war. If there was a campaign

for her countrymen, it was one
against sin. Musically
they were conscripted to proclaim

Sunday after Sunday the year
round they were on God's side. England
meanwhile detected its enemies

from afar. These made friends

out in the fields because
of its halo with the ancestral scarecrow.

Has she waited all these years
for me to forget myself
and do her homage? I begin
now: Ann Thomas, Ann Griffiths,
one of a thousand Anns chosen
to confound your parentage
with your culture — I know
Powys, the leafy backwaters
it is easy for the spirit to forget
its destiny in and put on soil
for its crown. You walked solitary
there and were not tempted,
or took your temptation as calling
to see Christ rising in April
out of that same soil and clothing
his nakedness like a tree. Your similes
were agricultural and profound.
As winter is forgiven by spring's
blossom, so defoliated man,
thrusting his sick hand in the earth's
side is redeemed by conviction.
Ann, dear, what can our scholarship
do but wander like Efyrnwy
your grass library, wondering at the absence
of all volumes but one? The question
teases us like the undying
echo of an Amen high up
in the cumulus rafters over Dolanog.

The theologians disagree
on their priorities. For her
the centuries' rhetoric contracted
to the three-letter word. What was sin

but the felix culpa enabling
a daughter of the soil to move
in divine circles? This was before
the bomb, before the annihilation
of six million Jews. It appears now
the confession of a child before
an upholstered knee; her achievement
the sensitising of the Welsh
conscience to the English rebuke.
The contemporary miracle is the feeding
of the multitude on the sublime
mushroom, while the Jesus,
who was her lover, is a face
gathering moss on the gable
of a defunct chapel, a myth shifting
its place to the wrong end
of the spectrum under the Doppler
effect of the recession of our belief.

Three pilgrimages to Bardsey
equalling one to Rome – How close
need a shrine be to be too far
for the traveller of today who is in
a hurry? Spare an hour or two
for Dolanog – no stone cross,
no Holy Father. What question
has the country to ask, looking as if
nothing has happened since the earth
cooled? And what is your question?
She was young and was taken.
If one asked you: 'Are you glad
to have been born?' would you let
the positivist reply for you
by putting your car in gear, or watch
the exuberance of nature in a lost
village, that is life saying Amen

to itself? Here for a few years
the spirit sang on a bone bough
at eternity's window, the flesh trembling
at the splendour of a forgiveness
too impossible to believe in, yet believing.

Are the Amens over? Ann (Gymraeg)
you have gone now but left us with the question
that has a child's simplicity and a child's depth:
Does the one who called to you,

when the tree was green, call us
also, if with changed voice,
now the leaves have fallen and the boughs
are of plastic, to the same thing?

    She listened to him.
    We listen to her.
    She was in time
    chosen. We but infer
    from the union of time
    with space the possibility
    of survival. She who was born
    first must be overtaken
    by our tomorrow.
    So with wings pinned
    and fuel rationed,
    let us put on speed
    to remain still
    through the dark hours
    in which prayer gathers
    on the brow like dew,
    where at dawn the footprints
    of one who invisibly
    but so close passed
    discover a direction.

from *The Echoes Return Slow* 1988

They keep me sober,
the old ladies
stiff in their beds,
mostly with pale eyes
wintering me.
Some are like blonde dolls
their joints twisted;
life in its brief play
was a bit rough.
Some fumble
with thick tongue for words,
and are deaf;
shouting their faint names
I listen;
they are far off,
the echoes return slow.

But without them,
without the subdued light
their smiles kindle,
I would have gone wild,
drinking earth's huge draughts
of joy and woe.

There are nights that are so still
that I can hear the small owl calling
far off, and a fox barking
miles away. It is then that I lie
in the lean hours awake, listening
to the swell born somewhere in the Atlantic
rising and falling, rising and falling
wave on wave on the long shore
by the village, that is without light
and companionless. And the thought comes
of that other being who is awake, too,
letting our prayers break on him
not like this for a few hours,
but for days, years, for eternity.

I have waited for him
    under the tree of science,
and he has not come;
    and no voice has said:
Behold a scientist in whom
    there is no guile.

I have put my hand in my pocket
    for a penny for the engaging
of the machinery of things and
    it was a bent
penny, fit for nothing but for placing
    on the cobbled eyeballs
of the dead.
            And where do I go
    from here? I have looked in
through the windows of their glass
    laboratories and seen them plotting
the future, and have put a cross
    there at the bottom
of the working out of their problems to
    prove to them that they were wrong.

from *Counterpoint* 1990

1. BC.

No, in the beginning was silence
that was broken by the word
forbidding it to be broken.

Hush: the sound of a bird landing
on water; sound of a thought
on time's shore; practice of Ur-language

by the first human. An echo
in God's mind of a conceived
statement. The sound of a rib

being removed out of the side
of the androgynous hero. The mumbling
of the Host by reptilian

lips. The shivering of love's
mirror as truth's frost
begins mercilessly to take hold.

It was a time when sparrows
lifted their voices above
the nightingales. The lonely
ones sang to their

aloneness; the audiences
were the sparrows'. Autumn
arrived; the nightingales
migrated. The sparrows died off

in their myriads. The frost
chirruped in places
where they had sat fast. From
bone galleries the audiences

had gone. In the hot south
featherless shadows fell
upon ruined cities that had never
heard the nightingales sing.

That was life's mischief
to create a plough
with no arable for it;
a chair without

a professor; twins the product
of no womb; a glittering
hunter but in need of
a quarry. And all as though

over our heads. Wiser
the Buddha who, though he looked
long, had no name for the packed
bud never to become a flower.

I know him.
He is the almost anonymous,
the one with the near perfect
alibi, the face over us that lacks
nothing but an expression.
He is the shape in the mist
on the mountain we would ascend
disintegrating as we compose it.

He can outpace us
in our pursuit, outdistancing
time only to disappear
in a black hole. He acknowledges
our relationship in the modes of thought
repudiating, when we would embody
thought in language, a syntactical
compulsion to incorporate
him in the second person.

I woke up
looked through the eye
of the needle of the rich
man found the view
to my taste climbed into
the tree of the knowledge
of good and evil to add
to my stature stood
in my own light admiring
my shadow and one
spoke to me there of
my one talent urging
investment the usury
of the spirit but I looked
out over the wall
of the garden where grapes grew
upon thorns and the machine gathered them and the dentures
of the children were not set on edge.

God smiled. The controls
were working: the small
eaten by the large, the large
by the larger. One problem
remained: the immunity
of a species. 'Easy,'
the jester at his side
whispered, indicating
the air's window that the germs
thronged. God opened it
a crack, and the human edifice
was dismantled. Among the ruins
one, stupider than the rest,
sat, seeing history's wheel
idle, putting a hand out, ready
to start it all over again.

There is a being, they say,
neither body nor spirit,
that is more power than reason, more reason
than love, whose origins
are unknown, who is apart
and with us, the silence
to which we appeal, the architect
of our failure. It takes the genes
and experiments with them and our children
are born blind, or seeing have
smooth hands that are the instruments
of destruction. It is the spoor
in the world's dark leading away
from the discovered victim, the expression
the sky shows us after
an excess of spleen. It has gifts it
distributes to those least fitted
to use them. It is everywhere and
nowhere, and looks sideways into the shocked face
of life, challenging it to disown it.

'As bubbles,' one said,
      'in the great bowl
of the sky; they come
      into being, they endure,
they explode. As are
      the stars, so we, but
our shining goes on
      in the great memory
and time makes us again:
      the body that is our shirt
of flame is re-woven and
      we wear it for joy
that through it an identity
      can appear. Ah, love,
whose property we believe
      is to outlast the burning,
be more than mineral in us,
      more than a spark
from the bush of the imagination
      we have set on fire.'

2. *Incarnation*

Top left an angel
hovering. Top right the attendance
of a star. From both
bottom corners devils
look up, relishing
in prospect a divine
meal. How old at the centre
the child's face gazing
into love's too human
face, like one prepared
for it to have its way
and continue smiling?

BEAUTY (upside down)   SATAN

A N G E L S   TRUTH (descending)

The Nativity? No.
Something has gone wrong.
There is a hole in the stable
acid rain drips through
onto an absence. Beauty
is hoisted upside down.
The truth is Pilate not
lingering for an answer.
The angels are prostrate
'beaten into the clay'
as Yeats thundered. Only
Satan beams down,
poisoning with fertilisers
the place where the child
lay, harrowing the ground
for the drumming of the machine-
gun tears of the rich that are
seed of the next war.

Other incarnations, of course,
consonant with the environment
he finds himself in,
animating the cells,
sharpening the antennae,
becoming as they are
that they, in the transparency
of their shadows, in the filament
of their calculations, may,
in their own way, learn to confront
the intellect with its issue.

And his coming testified
to not by one star
arrested temporarily
over a Judaic manger,
but by constellations innumerable
as dew upon surfaces
he has passed over time
and again, taking to himself
the first-born of the imagination
but without the age-old requirement of blood.

3. Crucifixion

God's fool, God's jester
capering at his right hand
in torment, proving the fallacy
of the impassible, reminding
him of omnipotence's limits.

I have seen the figure
on our human tree, burned
into it by thought's lightning
and it writhed as I looked.

A god has no alternative
but himself. With what crown
plurality but with thorns?
Whose is the mirthless laughter
at the beloved irony
at his side? The universe over,
omniscience warns, the crosses
are being erected from such
material as is available
to remorse. What are the stars
but time's fires going out
before ever the crucified
can be taken down?
                    Today
there is only this one option
before me. Remembering,
as one goes out into space,
on the way to the sun,
how dark it will grow,

I stare up into the darkness
of his countenance, knowing it
a reflection of the three days and nights
at the back of love's looking-
glass even a god must spend.

They set up their decoy
in the Hebrew sunlight. What
for? Did they expect
death to come sooner
to disprove his claim
to be God's son? Who
can shoot down God?
Darkness arrived at
midday, the shadow
of whose wing? The blood
ticked from the cross, but it was not
their time it kept. It was no
time at all, but the accompaniment
to a face staring,
as over twenty centuries
it has stared, from unfathomable
darkness into unfathomable light.

4. *AD.*

To be alive then
was to be aware how necessary
prayer was and impossible.

The philosophers had done
their work well, demolishing
proofs we never believed in.

We were drifting in space-
time, in touch with what we had
left and could not return to.

We rehearsed the excuses
for the deficiencies of love's
kingdom, avoiding our eyebeams.

Beset, as we were,
with science's signposts, we whimpered
to no purpose that we were lost.

We are here still. What
is survival's relationship
with meaning? The answer once

was the bone's music at the lips
of time. We are incinerating
them both now in the mind's crematorium.

The withholding
even of a request
that he remark my
silence: that was prayer.

I waited upon
him as a mirror
in its anonymity
waits upon absence.

Time passed. Once
from the closeness
of the invisible,
or in the after-draught

of the far-off, hurrying
about the immensity
of his being, I rose brimming
towards him like the spring-tide.

'The body is mine and the soul is mine'
says the machine. 'I am at the dark source
where the good is indistinguishable
from evil. I fill my tanks up
and there is war. I empty them
and there is not peace. I am the sound,
not of the world breathing, but
of the catch rather in the world's breath.'

Is there a contraceptive
for the machine, that we may enjoy
intercourse with it without being overrun
by vocabulary? We go up
into the temple of ourselves
and give thanks that we are not
as the machine is. But it waits
for us outside, knowing that when
we emerge it is into the noise
of its hand beating on the breast's
iron as Pharisaically as ourselves.

'Make my voice sharp
so it may rise to the clerestories
and pierce the ear
of the great God. And make
my sword sharp to enter
into the bowels of God's foes.'

Forget it. The Middle Ages
are over. On a bone
altar, with radiation
for candle, we make sacrifice
to the god of quasars
and pulsars, wiping
our robotic hands clean
on a disposable conscience.

Lord of the molecule and the atom
are you Lord of the gene, too?

An ancestor mingled his sperm
with the ovum and here is a warped life.

Were they so wrong who thought, when
it thundered, you were in a rage?

What is it, when the sky twitches
with lightning, but mimicry of your grimace?

I have seen the jay, that singer
out of tune, helping itself

to a morsel out of the lark's nest,
and you beamed down imperturbably as the sun.

We are used by the bacteria.
I have known the Chattertons and the Keats'

acting as porters of their obscene luggage.
What makes you God but the freedom

you have given us to bellow our defiance
at you over the grave's maw, or to let

silence ensue so deliberately
as to be taken for an Amen.

You show me two faces,
that of a flower opening
and of a fist contracting
like the gripping of ice.

You speak to me with two
voices, one thundering
on the ear's drum, the other
one mistakeable for silence.

Father, I said, domesticating
an enigma; and as though
to humour me you came.
But there are precipices

within you. Mild and dire,
now and absent, like us but
wholly other – which side
of you am I to believe?

He is that great void
we must enter, calling
to one another on our way
in the direction from which
he blows. What matter
if we should never arrive
to breed or to winter
in the climate of our conception?

Enough we have been given wings
and a needle in the mind
to respond to his bleak north.

There are times even at the Pole
when he, too, pauses in his withdrawal
so that it is light there all night long.

On an evening like this
the furies have receded.
There are only the shining sentinels
at hand: Yeats in his tower,
who was his own candle,
poring over the manuscript
of his people, discovering pride
in defeat; discovering the lidless
eye that beholds the beast
and the virgin. Edward Llwyd,
finding the flower that grew
nowhere but in Wales,
teaching us to look for rare things
in high places. Owain Glyndŵr
who tried blowing that flower
into flame in the memory
of an oppressed nation. The poets,
all of them, in all languages,
pausing on their migration
between thought and word
to watch here with me now
the moon come to its fifteenth phase
from whose beauty and madness
men have withdrawn these last days,
hand on heart, to its far
side of sanity and darkness.

There must be the mountain
receiving its degree
in purple and ermine;

and the girl with the drained face
moving the beholder
to ecstasy and grief.

There must be the skull
with spectacles on it
seeing what none see,

and the fly in the web
with its decibels of music
not attained to before.

All these must be there
as so many threads
of the garment without seam.

And to enthral the journey
that has no ending, once in a while
the falling of his shadow.

Madness? Its power
is to be recognised by the sane.
The insane ignore it.

They are busy with shells,
flowers, the difficulty
of discovering whose face it is

grimacing at them in the mirror.
There is no certainty
that we die when we are dead.

Maybe Dante was right;
maybe hell is inversion,
the becoming an inmate

of the paradise of the insane.
Manacled with equations,
foaming poetry at the mouth,

we will stare through the bones' bars
at those staring in, doing the mind's
trick over and over again to amuse them.

The imperatives of the instincts
in abeyance, heart and mind
at one in their contemplation
of the ripening apple never

to fall from the topmost branches
of truth's tree. A site for the repair
of promises that were broken, for picking
up pieces of the smashed dream.

It has the freshness of mushrooms,
proof of the whiteness darkness
can bring forth. It is the timeless
place, the unaccommodated

moment; an interval in the performance
of an unheard music. Do not believe
those who have been everywhere
but here. Tell the poor of the world

there is nothing to pay, no distance
to travel; that they are invited
to the marriage of here and now;
that the crystal in which they look,

grey with foreboding as the moon
with earth's shadow, has this
as its far side, turning necessarily towards
us with the reversal of our values.

When we are weak, we are
strong. When our eyes close
on the world, then somewhere
within us the bush

burns. When we are poor
and aware of the inadequacy
of our table, it is to that
uninvited the guest comes.

I think that maybe
I will be a little surer
of being a little nearer.
That's all. Eternity
is in the understanding
that that little is more than enough.

from *Mass for Hard Times* 1992

Mass for Hard Times

Kyrie

Because we cannot be clever and honest
and are inventors of things more intricate
than the snowflake – Lord have mercy.

Because we are full of pride
in our humility, and because we believe
in our disbelief – Lord have mercy.

Because we will protect ourselves
from ourselves to the point
of destroying ourselves – Lord have mercy.

And because on the slope to perfection,
when we should be half-way up,
we are half-way down – Lord have mercy.

Gloria

From the body at its meal's end
and its messmate whose meal is beginning,
                                        Gloria.

From the early and late cloud, beautiful and deadly
as the mushroom we are forbidden to eat,

                Gloria.

From the stars that are but as dew
and the viruses outnumbering the star clusters,

                Gloria.

From those waiting at the foot of the helix
for the rope-trick performer to come down,

                Gloria.

Because you are not there
When I turn, but are in the turning,

                Gloria.

Because it is not I who look
but I who am being looked through,

                Gloria.

Because the captive has found the liberty
that eluded him while he was free,

                Gloria.

Because from the belief that nothing is nothing
it follows that there must be something,

                Gloria.

Because when we count we do not count
the moment between youth and age,

                Gloria.

And because, when we are overcome,
we are overcome by nothing,

                Gloria.

Credo

I believe in God
the Father (Is he married?)
I believe in you, the almighty,
who can do anything
you wish. (Forget that irony
of the imponderable.) Rid, therefore
(if there are not too many
of them), my intestine
of the viruses that against
(in accordance with? Ah, horror!)
your will are in occupation
of its defences. I call
on you, as I have done
often before (why repeat,
if he is listening?) to show
you are master of secondary
causation. (What has physics to do
with the heart's need?) Am I
too late, then, with my language?
Are symbols to be in future
the credentials of our approach?
(And how contemporary
is the Cross, that long-bow drawn
against love?) My questions
accumulate in the knowledge
it is words are the kiss of Judas
that must betray you.
                              (My
parentheses are exhausted.) Almighty
pseudonym, grant me at last,
as the token of my belief,
such ability to remain
silent, as is the nearest to a reflection

of your silence to which
the human looking-glass may attain.

Sanctus

The bunsen flame burns and is not consumed,
and the scientist has not removed his shoes
because the ground is not holy.

And because the financiers' sun
is not Blake's sun, there is a
word missing from the dawn chorus.

Yet without subsidies poetry
sings on, celebrating the heart
and the 'holiness of its affections'.

And one listens and must not listen
in vain for the not too clinical
sanctus that is as the halo of its transplanting.

Benedictus

Blessed be the starved womb
and the replete womb.

Blessed the slug in the dew
and the butterfly among the ash-cans.

Blessed the mind that brings forth good and bad
and the hand that exonerates it.

Blessed be the adder among its jewels
and the child ignorant of how love must pay.

Blessed the hare who, in a round
world, keeps the tortoise in sight.

Blessed the cross warning: No through road,
and that other Cross with its arms out pointing both ways.

Blessed the woman who is amused
at Adam feeling for his lost rib.

Blessed the clock with its hands over its face
pretending it is midday, when it is midnight.

Blessed be the far side of the Cross and the back
of the mirror, that they are concealed from us.

Agnus Dei

No longer the Lamb
but the idea of it.
Can an idea bleed?
On what altar
does one sacrifice an idea?

It gave its life
for the world? No,
it is we give our life
for the idea that nourishes
itself on the dust in our veins.

God is love. Where
there is no love, no God?
There is only the gap between
word and deed we try
narrowing with an idea.

One Day

In that day language
shall expose its sores,
begging for the alms
we can not give. 'Leave it'
we shall say, 'on the pavement
of the quotidian.' There is
a cause there is nobody
to plead, yet whose sealed lips
are its credentials. What
does the traveller to your door
ask, but that you sit down
and share with him that
for which there are no words?
I look forward to the peace
conferences of the future
when lies, hidden behind speeches,
shall have their smiles blown away
by the dove's wings, fanning in silence.

Requests

To the angel without wings:
'Greetings; don't let me keep you.'

To the winged one, making as if
to be up and gone: 'Stay awhile.'

To the dark angel, pedlar
of reflections: 'I am not at home.'

To the one sworn eternally
to silence: 'Eavesdrop my heart.'

To truth's angel: 'In his ear about me
nothing but the white lie.'

Questions to the Prophet

How will the lion remain a lion
if it eat straw like the ox?

Where will the little child lead them
who has not been there before?

With our right hand off, with what
shall we beg forgiveness in the kingdom?

How shall the hare know it has not won,
dying before the tortoise arrive?

Did Christ crying: 'Neither do I condemn thee',
condemn the prostitute to be good for nothing?

If he who increases riches increases sorrow
why are his tears more like pearls than the swine's tusks?

Retired

Not to worry myself any more
if I am out of step, fallen behind.
Let the space probes continue;
I have a different distance to travel.

Here I can watch the night sky,
listen to how one grass blade
grates on another as member
of a disdained orchestra.

There are no meetings to attend
now other than those nocturnal
gatherings, whose luminaries
fell silent millenia ago.

No longer guilty of wasting
my time, I take my place
by a lily-flower, believing
with Blake that when God comes

he comes sometimes by way
of the nostril. My failure, perhaps,
was to have had no sense of smell
for the holiness suspiring from forked humans.

I count over the hours put by
for repentance, pulling thought's buildings
down to make way for the new,
fooling myself with the assurance

that when he occurs it is as the weather
of prayer's forecast, never with all
the unexpectedness of his body's
lightning, naked upon a cross.

The Reason

I gird myself for the agon.
And there at the beginning
is the word. What does it mean
and who initiated it?
Behind the word is the name
not to be known for fear
we should gain power over it.
It is buried under the page's
drift, and not all our tears,
not all our air-conditioning
can bring on the thaw. Our sentences
are but as footprints arrested
indefinitely on its threshold.

Perhaps our letters for it
are too many. Nearer the sound,
neither animal nor human,
drawn out through the wrenched
mouth of the oracle at Delphi.
Nearer the cipher the Christ
wrote on the ground, with no one
without sin to peer at it
over his shoulder.
                    Male
as I am, my place, perhaps,
is to sit down in a mysterious
presence, leaving the vocabularies
to toil, the machine to eviscerate
its resources; learning we are here
not necessarily to read on,

but to explore with blind
fingers the word in the cold,
until the snow turn to feathers
and somewhere far down we come
upon warmth and a heart beating.

Plas-yn-Rhiw

By day it is its own
audience. By night
its lights turn
to sores in the mist.

I have eavesdropped it
too long. It has nothing
to teach but that time
is the spirit's privation.

Memories are voracious.
What is left of my
life after, each day,
they have had their meal?

Morning or evening
up and down between
box on the worn
carpet of my patience.

Faces on long stems
remind. Bird voices
recall, charitable but
shrill . . . the velvet band

round the throat purring
with complacence. The place
itself is a memorial
to the peremptoriness

of emotions I have nothing
to bring to but pressed
flowers. The century
closes. The writing

of the lichen is too slow
for mind to attend
to. The sky modernises
its cipher and the orchard

where time dozed is
a laboratory for experimenting
with life's seed, where chromosomes
are divided, genes crossed

with genes, and God
shuts his eyes for mutations
to come up with a new
colouring for thought's apple.

Preference

The mythology of a species:
Jesus Christ? Muhamad? But only
the wind is real. We have tried
personalising it as divine breath,

but the answer of the universe
is 'OM! OM!' I have visited
the nurseries, seen childhood
revelling among tame

toys. Outside were the stars
that made shapes before
language began. The scientists teach
the possibility of thinking

without words. Their god
is the old nameless god
of calculus and inertia.
I understand rounded space,

time that is irreversible.
I have wakened in the night,
my hair rising at the passing
of presences that were not human;

switched on the light on articles
and upholstery, and switched it as soon
off in preference for the dark places
to the certainty of our domestication.

Aside

Cold beach, solitary
sea with its monotone
on the shingle; the ring
in the rock prohibiting
the conviction that no one
has been here before.

Man, is there anywhere
you can say this, peering
into the future under
the mushroom cloud? Mixed
with our oldest bones are
disturbing relics, too contemporary
to be there. In pre-history
someone came to this threshold
on which you hesitate
and crossed it, incinerating
the planet, leaving it
to life to lick its wounds
thousands of years. Thought
is as fast as light,
to exceed that brings annihilation
upon us.
            Yet wisdom
is at our elbow, whispering,
as at his once: Progress
is not with the machine;
it is a turning aside,
a bending over a still pool,
where the bubbles arise
from unseen depths, as from truth
breathing, showing us by their roundness
the roundness of our world.

Hark

You were wrong, Narcissus.
The replica of the self
is to be avoided. Echo
was right, warning you against

the malevolence of mirrors.
Yet the scientist still bends
over his cloning, call as she may,
irrefutable beside the gene-pool.

The Refusal

First it was gilled man,
then man quadruped,
man erect, peering
without recognising it
at his future. Losing trust
in the present he invented
the chronometer to go faster.
Mobile man, wheeled man,
man trying to keep up
with himself. Vocabulary toiled
behind science, behind music,
the brush.
       I have seen
the winged man, and he was no
angel. Was there a turning
he missed, where resources
could have been stored
by watching without envy
the directionless accelerations?

There is no answer other
than that it is too late to be saved
by the multitude of our questions.
Begrudging us our tenancy
of a remote peace, they make
our periphery their centre
through speed and noise. Wringing
our hands, we wring our belief
dry, refusing from pride
or shame after the failure
of our specifics the one cultivable
remedy the intellect disdains.

Tidal

The waves run up the shore
and fall back. I run
up the approaches of God
and fall back. The breakers return
reaching a little further,
gnawing away at the main land.
They have done this thousands
of years, exposing little by little
the rock under the soil's face.
I must imitate them only
in my return to the assault,
not in their violence. Dashing
my prayers at him will achieve
little other than the exposure
of the rock under his surface.
My returns must be made
on my knees. Let despair be known
as my ebb-tide; but let prayer
have its springs, too, brimming,
disarming him; discovering somewhere
among his fissures deposits of mercy
where trust may take root and grow.

Match My Moments

That time
the soldier broke in
to my room and I,
the sword at my throat,
looked up from my sums
and theorems and smiling
said: Spare my designs.

That time
in the rusting bracken
the road ran with sheep,
a woollen river but vocal,
saying in its raw baritone
to the man on its banks:
We give our life for the shepherd.

That time
the queue winding towards
the gas chambers, and the nun,
who had already died
to this world, to the girl
in tears: Don't cry. Look,
I will take your place.

That time
after the night's frost the tree
weeping, the miser in me
complaining: Why all this washing
the earth's feet in gold? And I,
my finger at my lips: Because
it is what we are made of.

Healing

Sick wards. The sailed beds
becalmed. The nurses tack
hither and fro. The chloroform
breeze rises and falls.
Hospitals are their own
weather. The temperatures
have no relation
to the world outside. The surgeons,
those cunning masters
of navigation, follow
their scalpels' compass through
hurricanes of pain to a calm
harbour. Somewhere far down
in the patient's darkness,
where faith died, like a graft
or a transplant prayer
gets to work, repairing
the soul's tissue, leading
the astonished self between
twin pillars, where life's angels
stand wielding their bright swords of flame.

Markers

Wittgenstein's signposts pointing
at the boundaries of language
into the obligatory void.

Laplace, hypothetically
unembarrassed, the self-made thinker's
bravado in front of a condescension.

Hume, bumping his mind
so often against a cause,
as to become insensible of its presence.

Descartes thinking he could think
Descartes, but what he thought were
the co-respondents in a divorce.

Buridan's ass? No, a catalepsy
of time at the thought of the narrowing
of the interval between two mouthfuls.

To where it began: Plato jilting
the one truth at his side for the shadowless
idea of it ogling him from Parnassus.

Eschatology

It was our last inter-glacial:
the flies, people,
the one as numerous
as the other. We talked
peace, and brought our arms up to date.
The young ones professed
love, embarrassing themselves
with their language. As though
coming round on a new
gyre, we approached God
from the far side, an extinct concept.
No one returned from our space
probes, yet still there were
volunteers, believing that as
gravity slackened its hold
on the body, so would time
on the mind. Our scientists,
immaculately dressed not
conceived, preached to us
from their space-stations, calling us
to consider the clockwork birds
and fabricated lilies, how they
also, as they were conditioned to
do, were neither toiling nor spinning.

The Un-born

I have seen the child in the womb,
neither asking to be born
or not to be born, biding its time
without the knowledge of time,
model for the sculptor who would depict
the tranquillity that inheres
before thought, or the purity of thought
without language. Its smile forgave
the anachronism of the nomenclature
that would keep it foetal. Its hands
opened delicately as flowers
in innocency's garden, ignorant
of the hands growing to gather them
for innocency's grave.
Was its part written? I have seen
it waiting breathlessly in the wings
to come forth on to a stage
of soil or concrete, where wings
are a memory only or an aspiration.

Sure

Where the lamb died
a bird sings.
Where a soul perishes
what music? The cross

is an old-fashioned
weapon, but its bow
is drawn unerringly
against the heart.

254

Time

The pessimist says: Time
goes; the optimist: It is coming.

What is this thing, time?
Let Augustine be our spokesman.

Its competitor knows its neurosis;
the lover the dragging of its chained feet.

Now, we say, looking at the moon
that is the sun in Australia.

We keep saving it for the future
and arriving there are insolvent.

Young, our hobby was assassinating it.
Old we pray for its recuperation.

Something More

You remain contented
    with your anonymity.
We ask for survival
      for John Jones.
We acknowledge the tree
    that at moments
you are ablaze in,
      taking our shoes
off, involuntarily remembering
there is dung at its roots.

They say there is a pool
    at the bottom of which
you lie, and that we ourselves
      are the troublers
of its surface. But why,
    when we look down,
      is it as though
we looked up at our own faces
at home there among the cloud branches?

Target

I look up at the sky at night
and see the archer, Sagittarius,
with his bow drawn, and realise
man is the arrow speeding,

not as some think infinitely
on, but because space is curved,
backwards towards the bowman's heart
to deal him his unstanched wound.

The Seasons

Spring

The spirit sang on the bone
to the blood that was in
me, and many as flowers
thought seeded and grew
words in the mind's garden –
the promise of language!
I was the poet coming
to it for its nectar. I fed
full on the ambivalences of honey.
I built high in my branches,
augury of a serene summer.
Love fledged and was no migrant
but resident and identified
by the unreasonableness of its music.

Summer

Everywhere pattern;
design without a designer?
I gather a bird's feather
which looks at me in
silence and tells all.

In every member of
its species the same eye
will be found in the same
barbules, saying nothing,
informing us who it is.

It is the summer of
the plumage. Like fruit

ripening, ready to fall,
the feather brightens towards
harvest and lets go.

There is an August
within us, aeons
of preparation for a few
kingfisher days. We fly
the diameter of a circle.

She was the colour
of corn. Fine wheat
was her texture. Somewhere
within her, palpitating,
was the heart's poppy.

Autumn

Happy the leaves
burnishing their own
downfall. Life dances
upon life's grave.
It is we who inject
sadness into the migrant's
cry. We are so long
in dying – time granted
to discover a purpose
in our decay? Could
we be cut open,
would there be more than
the saw's wound, all
humanity's rings widening
only towards ageing?
To creep in for shelter
under the bone's tree
is to be charred by time's

lightning stroke. The leaves
fall variously as do thoughts
to reveal the bareness
of the mind's landscape
through which we must press on
towards the openness of its horizons.

Winter

The machine is
our winter, smooth
as ice glassing
over the soul's surface.

We have looked
it in the eye
and seen how our image
gradually is demoted.

Without the tribute
we must bring it
from our dwindling resources
it grows colder and colder.

It is our January
and our December,
a two-faced God
on an unreal threshold

directing its eyes back
at the hand's blindness,
but forward also towards
the defeat of time.

Pen Llŷn

Dafydd looked out;
I look out: five centuries
without change? The same sea breaks
on the same shore and is not
broken. The stone in Llŷn
is still there, honey-
coloured for a girl's hair
to resemble. It is time's
smile on the cliff
face at the childishness
of my surprise. Here was the marriage
of land and sea, from whose bickering
the spray rises. 'Are you there?'
I call into the dumb
past, that is close to me
as my shadow. 'Are you here?'
I whisper to the encountered
self like one coming
on the truth asleep
and fearing to disturb it.

A Marriage

We met
　　under a shower
of bird-notes.
　　Fifty years passed,
love's moment
　　in a world in
servitude to time.
　　She was young;
I kissed with my eyes
　　closed and opened
them on her wrinkles.
　　'Come' said death,
choosing her as his
　　partner for
the last dance. And she,
　　who in life
had done everything
　　with a bird's grace,
opened her bill now
　　for the shedding
of one sigh no
　　heavier than a feather.

What Then?

You chose the natural timber
to die on that the natural
man should be saved. What boughs,
then, will need to be crossed
and what body crucified
upon them for salvation
to be won for the astronauts
venturing in their air-conditioned
capsules? Will artificial living
give birth to the artificial
sin? What prayers will they say
upside down in their space-chambers?
Are you prepared to reveal
the nuclear brain and the asbestos
countenance to deserve their worship?
They are planning their new conurbations
a little nearer the stars,
incinerated by day and by night
glacial; but will there be room there
for a garden for the Judas
of the future to make his way through
to give you his irradiated kiss?

Newts

In a pool
on the mountain
newts live, semi-
palmated, grey-faced
as stone; reptilian
gargoyles on cornices
of water. Their world
stretches from horizon
to horizon, which is
two feet by two.
                    Here
everything happens:
pain, bliss, hunger –
but what are a newt's
thoughts? Their brows corrugated
from long pondering
a scaled truth they rest
panting like life itself
on the wondering journey
that is without end.

The Lost

Mourners after the shadows
they are deprived of
by an absence of light.

Speak to them, they will not
hear. Write them letters,
they will not receive them.

Their address is the darkness
behind the mirrors
their captors confront us with.

They are nothing, nobody,
sunk to their knees not
in prayer; mouths opening

not for converse, for offal
the guards administer them
with to prolong their anguish.

Go your way. Comfort
yourself with the reminder
you can do nothing.

They are beyond the reach
even of an Amen. The Grand
Inquisitor's countenance

is averted. Jesus'
too? The bread of the one
and the freedom of the other

offer no more light
to the nameless than does
the mildew forming upon both.

Afon Rhiw

Its methods were not sweeping
away, but by a continual plucking
to make one lose one's hold
on its stones. Its character
was that of thought: smooth
brow with behind it the trout
rising and disappearing swiftly
as an idea. I angled
for them, dandling a fly
between one depth and another,
hoping for the mandala
to come to the surface to concentrate
the mind. What is existence
but standing patiently for a while
amid flux? Mostly the fish
nibbled and were gone, singing
mistily out of my reach.
The fly soared, drying its wings
in the March wind before
redoubling its temptations,
offering like life itself
a hook hidden among feathers.

Let me tell you that without
catching a thing I was not far
from the truth that time, since meaning
is not in having but trying.
Questioned, the trout had confessed
I was indistinguishable
from a tree, roots in darkness
my head in the clouds, and that

like thoughts, too, their best place
was among the shadows rather
than being drawn into the light's
dryness to perish of too much air.

Sonata in X

ADAM: 'What's that you've got on?'
EVE: 'Nothing. Why?'
ADAM: 'I could have sworn.'
EVE: 'Don't do that. Here, taste.'
ADAM: 'H'm! Who gave it you?'
EVE: 'He flowed. Look – like this.'
ADAM: 'Whereas I am erect, rigid.
　　　But listen ... What's that?'

Some said: 'The voice of a god.'
And others, it thundered.
Ever since then two
minds, and reason between them,
pendulum of a stopped
clock. If what is true
is not fair, how can
what is fair, then, be true?

　I woke up
　looked through the eye
　of the needle of the rich
　man found the view
　to my taste climbed into
　the tree of the knowledge
　of good and evil to add
　to my stature stood
　in my own light admiring
　my shadow and one
　spoke to me there of
　my one talent urging
　investment the usury
　of the spirit but I looked
　out over the wall

of the garden where grapes grew
upon thorns and the machine
gathered them so that the children's
dentures were not set on edge.

Waking and wondering
when was I and where
had I been? Standing back

from myself, beginning to recall
uterine experience,
an antiphonal music

in infinite counterpoint
between mirror and mirror.
Time was technology's

folk-tale. My introspection
could have been called a navel
engagement; the truth my ability

to hold all things in play;
bringing beauty to birth
out of my unbreached side.

My apostrophes were to myself
only. I found, when I leaned
closer, the second person

did not exist. Vertical in my
dimensionless presence I kept calling
to the undying echoes: 'Prove that I lie.'

There was something I was near
and never attained: a pattern,
an explanation. Why did I address it

in person? The evolutionists told
me I was wrong. My premises,
the philosophers assured me,
were incorrect. Perpendicular
I agreed, but on my knees
looking up, cap in hand,
at the night sky I laid astronomy
on one side. These were the spiritual
conurbations illuminated always
by love's breath; a colonising
of the far side of the mind
without loss of the openness of its spaces.

The foolish ones bred
   all the time,
the wise in the intervals
   between wars; their children came

to the same end. The poet took notice
   of this, but lacked rhyme
to express it, and his prosody
   was out of date. History

has nothing to teach, nor humanity
   to learn. Our lessons are done
out of school in the church-
   yard under the owl's cry.

Maggots, I thought, how like bread
they are, crumbled;
yet it is they who eat
us and not we them.

In flight's cause we perish.

There is a sacrament of death, too.

Arguing since Plato's
day: Does the tune exist
when the instruments are
silent? If we could solve

that, there would be nothing to do
but sing in the crab's ear,
beside the gene-pool, at the re-installed
tables of the money changers.

He never asked himself what was sin,
but, challenged, would have replied:
'The neutrality of the affections.'

He never enquired what was power,
but drank from it insatiably
as a looking-glass drinks at the conscience.

She never sought an argument
for behaviour but arrowed her glances
impenitently as her mood blew.

She was mixed ground for the sowing
of such seed as, grown tall, would
declare for righteousness and betray it.

What poet, scientist,
musician ever arrived

who was behind the times?
Last night I crept up on him

in the dark. This morning
there is only the bone's sand

with the footprints the oncoming
tide is erasing one by one.

    'I love you.'
    'How much?'
    '$1^{32} \times \sqrt{-1}$.'
    'Wait a minute, let me
    compute my thanks.
                     There.
    Meet me tonight
    at SH 126 243
    so we may
    consummate our statistics.'

Galileo's lens, so long idle,
has become the peep-hole
of time, crowded with faces,
voyeurs of the spirit's
adultery with the machine.

    See the black lightning
    of its tongue, followed
    by the thunder in my veins.
    Ah, bright god, so near

    to the ground, do you still tempt
    me from behind a flower
    to put out my glad hand
    for the toothsomeness that is anguish?

Man, two
million years at
his back – parvenu.

Kestrel,
older, arrested
permanently in its ascent.

Rock of
no age, its hundred-weights
fortuitously poised.

Now! Man,
car, rock in the high
pass keeping an appointment.

Witness?
The kestrel in the sky
burning, but not to tell.

from *No Truce with the Furies* 1995

Geriatric

What god is proud
   of this garden
of dead flowers, this underwater
   grotto of humanity,
where limbs wave in invisible
   currents, faces drooping
on dry stalks, voices clawing
   in a last desperate effort
to retain hold? Despite withered
   petals, I recognise
the species: Charcot, Ménière,
   Alzheimer. There are no gardeners
here, caretakers only
   of reason overgrown
by confusion. This body once,
   when it was in bud,
opened to love's kisses. These eyes,
   cloudy with rheum,
were clear pebbles that love's rivulet
   hurried over. Is this
the best Rabbi Ben Ezra
   promised? I come away
comforting myself, as I can,
   that there is another

garden, all dew and fragrance,
   and that these are the brambles
about it we are caught in,
   a sacrifice prepared
by a torn god to a love fiercer
   than we can understand.

Still Point

In the universe one
world beneath cloud
foliage. In that world
a town. In the town

a house with a child,
who is blind, staring
over the edge of the universe
into the depths of love.

Lunar

The moon never sets
in Northampton. Every time
I pass through it stares
at me from a window
of the asylum and is always
at the full. Don't be misled
by those likenesses of it
when it was new and shone
down on unenclosed meadows.
As it waxed it became
bald. It was a skull
where names chased one another
without end, wife and sweetheart
hurrying by like shadows
over the corn. For ignorance
time stops by a flower.
Young he was in his own
sky, rising at mornings
over unbrushed dew,
with no one to introduce
him to earth's bustling creatures
but his love. It was love
brought him, as it brings
all of us in the end, face
against glass, to demand
brokenly of the anonymous: Who am I?

The Pearl

'I think we have not,'
I said, 'been introduced.'

'No need,' it replied;
'I introduced myself

in the Garden, metallic
of scale, offering

the future to you in place
of the god's past. Would you

grow wings, anticipate
the clock? Behold, I am

at your door, in your
kitchen, at your bed's

side. I was the irritant
in the oyster that was

Leonardo's brain you have
split open to prove

to your conditioned audience
there is no pearl without price.'

Evening

The archer with time
as his arrow – has he broken
his strings that the rainbow
is so quiet over our village?

Let us stand, then, in the interval
of our wounding, till the silence
turn golden and love is
a moment eternally overflowing.

Then

The bone's song will be:
'Let me sleep. I am not
Yeats. I cannot face
over again the coming
of the machine. What was it
but a twig put in our hands
for the divining of the blood's
mineral within the marrow?'

And the one who is used
to ignoring prayer
will put the bone to his lips,
blowing it to the dust
that dances before
the galaxies, casting its veils
one by one to emerge
beautiful and deadly
as the nuclear core
that, Narcissus-like,
he gazes upon
as though it were a mirror.

Riposte

'A matter of chance?'
'All right for the lucky.

For those born blind,
those whom the crab

mumbles.' 'A design, then?'
'Not orientated manward.'

'Are you brave? Is life
but a sea, golden-

winged, moulting
upon our shores to

develop new feathers
for its meaningless returns?'

'You would persuade me
toward God.' 'What God?

Are we apparel
of his wardrobe, clothes

to be worn an hour
in a procession and cast off?'

'You make a mountain
of a concept. Why is there not

level ground, where
the rankness of evil

falls to our paternosters?'
'You derive vocabulary

from the Schoolmen.
Omnipotence is no answer

to secondary causation.'
'All right, I allow

you your mountain,
if you will allow

me that the cloud
at its summit is what

God withdraws into
at the moment of illumination.'

To a Lady

I don't know
who I write to,
the frocked girl,
pretty but pert,
or the grown-up
mother, doll-less
but dolled. Nor
does death either
who, liquidating
her lungs, applying
irons to her heart,
discovers, astonished,
a being somewhere
between both, perter
than a child, prettier
than a parent, and
wiser than each
of them in the way
she treats his fumbling
familiarity with contempt.

Afallon

It is Adam's other
kingdom, what he might have
inherited had he
refused the apple, the nuclear
fruit with the malignant core.
Its women trace their descent
not to Eve but to Lilith,
the spirit that whispers to us
when we take the world
in our arms. Standing
under the tree of man,
our roots in the soil, we listen
to Rhiannon's birds high
in the branches, calling to us
to forget time, so that the heart
answers: Its lichened manuscripts
of stone; its wind-laundered
clouds; the moving
staircases of its streams –
the traveller gets down
onto a midnight platform
and knows from the rustle
of unseen water-
falls he has come home.
Once our literature
was on the continent's
lips; we exchanged delegates
with its princes. In a world
oscillating between dollar
and yen our liquidities
are immaterial. We
continue our relationship
with the young David, flooring

the cheque-book giant
with one word taken,
smooth as a pebble, out
of the brook of our language.

Wrong?

Where is that place apart
you summon us to? Noisily
we seek it and have no time
to stay. Stars are distant;
is it more distant still,
out in the dark in the shadow
of thought itself? No wonder
it recedes as we calculate
its proximity in light years.

Maybe we were mistaken
at the beginning or took later
a wrong turning. In curved space
one can travel for ever and not recognise
one's arrivals. I feel rather
you are at our shoulder, whispering
of the still pool we could sit down
by; of the tree of quietness
that is at hand; cautioning us
to prepare not for the breathless journeys
into confusion, but for the stepping
aside through the invisible
veil that is about us into a state
not place of innocence and delight.

Meteorological

It was always weather.
The reason of our being
was to record it, telling it
how it was hot, cold, wet
to the pointlessness of saturation.
It was a disposition
of the impersonal, an expression
on what could have been
blank space. It repeated itself
in a way we were never tired
of listening to. 'Do that again,'
we implored it on the morrow
of a fine day. When it was grey
you could have described it
as sullen. On sparkling mornings
it flashed us smile after smile so
we became familiar with it.
It breathed then into our very being
refrigerating us. To curse it
was to have it regard us
out of the mildest of skies,
fondling us with the wind's
tapering fingers. They say
it was like this before
our arrival. How could it
have been without us
to convince it? What, when we
have gone, will become
of it, endlessly occurring
over our vocabulary's Sahara?

Reflections

The furies are at home
in the mirror; it is their address.
Even the clearest water,
if deep enough can drown.

Never think to surprise them.
Your face approaching ever
so friendly is the white flag
they ignore. There is no truce

with the furies. A mirror's temperature
is always at zero. It is ice
in the veins. Its camera
is an X-ray. It is a chalice

held out to you in
silent communion, where gaspingly
you partake of a shifting
identity never your own.

Incarnations

A child's memories
are of the womb, the sleep
by unearthly waters;
his dreams are of a happiness
unfounded. This one fell,
was torn out of a vast side
by envy in transit.
His whickering disordered
the stars, then silence took over,
twelve dawdling years
on the way to the temple.

    Take one from one
    there remain three.
    No, no, no.

    Through a child's answer
    a cross was drawn
    by Judaic fingers.

    The way forward
    was the way back
    to a carpenter's patience.

A preacher's temptation
is the voice persuading
he is his own message.
So the emphasis on the other
proved to them he blasphemed.
This stripling, this Nazarene
nobody the mirror
of God! They hurled their scorn's
stones and the cracks accentuated

the sky's age. There was scant time.
He withdrew into the wilderness
of the spirit. The true fast
was abstention from language.

    He returned hungry
    yet offered his body
    as bread to believers.

    The crumbs flew
    lavishing their feathers
    on twelve baskets.

    They lost him then
    in the garden of himself
    gloomy with prayer

    until Judas found him,
    enviously guided by the sour
    shining of his starved kiss.

What are a god's dreams?
Can he dream without sleep?
What was the Incarnation
but the waking dream of one
calling himself Son of Man?

For the dreams come, always they come:
the babe's dream by amniotic
waters; dream of the ovum
of the enchanted circle
when it was yet unpierced.

What are a child's dreams?
Bubbles blown for adults
to seek their reflections in?

R. S. THOMAS

What are the leaves in autumn
but the mind flaking beneath

truth's chisel? I have heard the professor,
laying his books down, huskily
describing the first rise
on a river in Scotland.
I have listened to the poet

with uncombed hair, delicate
of finger, adding nought
after nought to his imagined
balance. I have said to the future:
'Show me the dreamless man,

the prose man, the man imprisoned
by his horizons.' And the machine
stalled at an abyss, empty
as the tomb in Palestine,
the eternal afterdraught of the bone's dream.

At the End

Few possessions: a chair,
a table, a bed
to say my prayers by,
and, gathered from the shore,
the bone-like, crossed sticks
proving that nature
acknowledges the Crucifixion.
All night I am at
a window not too small
to be frame to the stars
that are no further off
than the city lights
I have rejected. By day
the passers-by, who are not
pilgrims, stare through the rain's
bars, seeing me as prisoner
of the one view, I who
have been made free
by the tide's pendulum truth
that the heart that is low now
will be at the full tomorrow.

A Species

Shipwrecked upon an island
in a universe whose tides
are the winds, they began multiplying
without joy. They cut down the trees
to have room to make money.

The one who is without name,
but all-powerful, sowed intelligence
in them like a virus. As living room
became scarce, as rain became acid,
they became conscious there were other islands

all round, garlands hung up
at the festivities of science,
waiting to be colonised not by
the imagination but in fact.
They learned how time can be superannuated

by speed, making an archipelago
of the stars, hurrying from one
to another with their infection.
There came a day when the one
without name and whose signature

is in cypher willed them to go back
to their first home, destitute but wiser.
They turned as to a familiar, seeing it
for the first time, suspended in beauty,
blue with cold, but waiting to be loved.

Near and Far

No one so busy
as you are. Where is that
seventh day when you rest
from your labour? I arise
from sleep to find that
you have been all night growing.
And by day you are abroad
endlessly exploring a circumference
by which you are not confined.
You have no words yet vibrate
in me with the resonance of an Amen.
You are strung with light
as with nerves across which
thought is drawn to deliver
intellectual music. Sometimes
you are an impulse upon my walls,
at others a modifying
of unseen organisms, slowly
and delicately as a mutation;
but always as far off
as you are near, terrifying
me as much by your proximity
as by your being light-years away.

Resurrections

Easier for them, God
only at the beginning
of his recession. Blandish him,
said the times and they did so,
Herbert, Traherne, walking
in a garden not yet
polluted. Music in Donne's
mind was still polyphonic.

The corners of the spirit waiting
to be developed, Hopkins
renewed the endearments
taming the lion-like presence
lying against him. What
happened? Suddenly he was
gone, leaving love guttering
in his withdrawal. And scenting
disaster, as flies are attracted
to a carcase, far down
in the subconscious the ghouls
and the demons we thought
we had buried for ever resurrected.

Winged God

All men. Or shall we say,
not chauvinistic, all
people, it is all
people? Beasts manure
the ground, nibble to
promote growth; but man,
the consumer, swallows
like the god of mythology
his own kind. Beasts walk
among birds and never
do the birds scare; but the human,
that alienating shadow
with the Bible under the one
arm and under the other
the bomb, as often
drawn as he is repelled
by the stranger waiting for him
in the mirror – how
can he return home
when his gaze forages
beyond the stars? Pity him,
then, this winged god, rupturer
of gravity's control
accelerating on and
outward in the afterglow
of a receding laughter?

R. S. THOMAS

Raptor

You have made God small,
setting him astride
a pipette or a retort
studying the bubbles,
absorbed in an experiment
that will come to nothing.

I think of him rather
as an enormous owl
abroad in the shadows,
brushing me sometimes
with his wing so the blood
in my veins freezes, able

to find his way from one
soul to another because
he can see in the dark.
I have heard him crooning
to himself, so that almost
I could believe in angels,

those feathered overtones
in love's rafters, I have heard
him scream, too, fastening
his talons in his great
adversary, or in some lesser
denizen, maybe, like you or me.

Incubation

In the absence of such wings
as were denied us we insist
on inheriting others from the machine.
The eggs that we incubate bring forth
in addition to saints monsters,
the featherless brood whose one thing
in common with dunnocks is
that they do not migrate. We are fascinated
by evil; almost you could say
it is the plumage we acquire
by natural selection. There is a contradiction
here. Generally subdued feathers
in birds are compensated for
by luxuriant song. Not so these
whose frayed notes go with their plain clothes.
It is we who, gaudy as jays,
make cacophonous music under an egg-shell sky.

Gwladus Ddu
(from the Welsh of G. J. Williams)

It was an old white-friar who wrote
on yellowing parchment among tales
of the Welsh princes these words:
'That year was buried Gwladus Ddu.'

What was it made a brother
in his cell insert this in his story?
Did he taste heaven once in seeing
the sun brighten the darkness of Gwladus Ddu?

And I, too, by my fireside remembered,
seeing Eryri's cover white as wool,
that seven hundred winters had grizzled it
since summer basked in the hair of Gwladus Ddu.

Just now behind the manuscript's account
of old, bold knights I saw a face
bloodless and unsmiling and the words:
'That year was buried Gwladus Ddu.'

Neither

Not a person, neither
less than, since we are so,
personal. Impassible
yet darkening your countenance
once for a long moment
as you looked at yourself
on a hill-top in Judea.
Your mastery is to be both
outside and inside, standing off
from the primary explosion,
entering in to its quieter
repetitions in acorn and spermatozoa.
You have given us the ability
to ask the unanswerable question,
to have glimpses of you
as you were, only to stand dumb
at the limits of our articulation.
Is it our music interprets you
best, a heart-beat at the very centre
of your creation? Is it art,
depicting man's figure as the conductor
to your lightning? Had I
the right words, it is the poem
that would announce you to
an amazed audience; no longer
a linguistic wrestling but a signal
projected at you and returning quick
with the unpredictabilities at your centre.

The Promise

Promising myself before bedtime
to contend more urgently
with the problem. From nothing
nothing comes. Behind everything –
something, somebody? In the beginning
violence, the floor of the universe
littered with fragments. After
that enormous brawl, where
did the dove come from? From what
acorn mind these dark
boughs among which at night
thought loses its way back
to its dim sources, onward
to that illuminated citadel
that truth keeps? Light's distances
are without meaning and unreconciled
by the domestic. I pit my furniture
against the emptiness that is beyond
Antares, but the equation
is not in balance. There are no cushions
for the emotions. Thermodynamic
cold or else incineration
of the planet – either way
there is no hope for the species.
Are Sophocles and Mozart sufficient
justification for the failure
to find out? Beyond
the stars are more stars where love, perhaps,
or intellect or the anonymous is busy.

Bird Watching

Choosing amid many whisperings
the enamel platitudes
of the Mediterranean; Sappho
and Propertius at it
to impinge on the *Telegraph*'s
stop press; to observe birds
their wavering italics
in competition with the ocean's
serene gaze. The post chaise
was a necessary adjunct
of the grand tour; we thumb
our way, our arrival
as unsuspected as an occurrence
of influenza. A thousand
binoculars winnow
the thin haze. Eyes
that in other places
would be penetrating
the young women's amorphous
clothing can here notice
the lack of cosmetics
that distinguish one warbler
from another. Winged God
approve that in a world
that has appropriated flight
to itself there are still people
like us, who believe
in the ability of the heart
to migrate, if only momentarily,
between the quotidian and the sublime.

Hallowe'en

Outside a surfeit of planes.
Inside the hunger of the departed
to come back. 'Ah, erstwhile humans,
would you make your mistakes
over again? In life, as in love,
the second time round is
no better.'
        I confront their expressions
in the embers, on grey walls:
faces among the stones watching
me to see if this night
of all nights I will make sacrifice
to the spirits of hearth and of
roof-tree, pouring a libation.

'Stay where you are,' I implore.
'This is no world for escaped beings
to make their way back into.
The well that you took your pails
to is polluted. At the centre
of the mind's labyrinth the machine howls
for the sacrifice of the affections;
vocabulary has on a soft collar
but the tamed words are not to be trusted.
As long as the flames hum, making
their honey, better to look in
upon truth's comb than to
take off as we do on fixed wings
for depollinated horizons.'

Navigation
(for Lee McOwan)

There go the storeyed liners,
the tankers, the thudding substitutes
for the billowing schooners
that were blown away as though
they were time's clouds. I wave
to them on their way – where?
They are, as I am, outward
bound over multitudinous
fathoms. The crew lean over
the taffrail, I over myself
and suffer the old nausea
of the unknown. Sometimes when there is
fog, I hear the horn calling
to them to be careful. When I
kneel down in the obscurity
that is God, there is no comparable
voice, however melancholy,
to direct me.
         Never mind,
traveller, there are the heights,
too, where the intellect
meets with God in its own
weather. By day I see the 'planes
reflecting him with the clarity
that is thought. By night
their instruments deputise
for him and are unerring.
God, on this latest stage
of my journey let me profit

from my inventions by christening
them yours. Amid the shoals and hazards
that are about me, let me employ
radar as though it were your gift.

Nant Gwrtheyrn

I listen to the echoes
of John Jones crying: 'God
is not good,' and of his wife
correcting him: 'Hush, John.'

'The cuckoo returns
to Gwrtheyrn, contradicting
John Jones, within its voice
bluebells tolling over

the blue sea. There is work
here still, quarrying
for an ancient language
to bring it to the light

from under the years'
dust covering it. Men,
with no palate for fine
words, they helped them down

with their sweat, spitting
them out later in what
served them for prayer. Was
it for this God numbered

their days? Where once pick-
axes would question, now
only the stream ticks, telling
a still time to listeners

at their text-books. Turning
its back on the world,
contemplating without boredom
unchanging horizons this place

knows a truth, for here
is the resurrection
of things. One after one
they arise in answer

to names they are called by,
standing around, shining,
by brief graves from whose hold
willing hands have released them.

Remembering

Love her now
        for her ecstasies,
her willingness to oblige.
There will come a time
she will show her love for you
            in her cooking,
her sewing; in a bed made up
        for passionless sleeping.

The wrinkles will come upon her
        calm though her brow be
under time's blowing. Frost will visit
        her hair's midnight and not
thaw. Her eyes that were a fine day
            will cloud over
        and rain down desultory
tears when, as she infers,
you are not looking. Your part then
will be to take her hand in your
        hand, proving to her
that, if blind, it is not dumb.

Island

I would still go there
if only to await
the once-in-a-lifetime
opening of truth's flower;

if only to escape
such bought freedom, and live,
prisoner of the keyless sea,
on the mind's bread and water.

Silence

The relation between us was
silence; that and the feeling
of each one being watched
by the other: I by an
enormous pupil in a blank
face, he by one in a million
wanderers in the darkness
that was never a long way off
from his presence.
              It had begun
by my talking all of the time
repeating the worn formulae
of the churches in the belief
that was prayer. Why does silence
suggest disapproval? The prattling
ceased, not suddenly but,
as flowers die off in a frost
my requests thinned. I contented
myself I was answering
his deafness with dumbness. My tongue
lolled, clapper of a disused
bell that would never again
pound on him.
              What are the emotions
of God? There was no admiring
of my restraint, no suggestion even
of a recompense for my patience.
If he had allowed himself but one
word: his name, for instance, spoken
ever so obliquely; my own that,
for all his majesty, acknowledged
my existence.
              And yet there were creatures

around me with their ears
pricked; figures on ancient cathedrals,
the denizens of art, with their rapt,
innocent faces and heads on one side
as though they were listening. Ah, but to whom?

Blind Noel

Christmas; the themes are exhausted.
Yet there is always room
on the heart for another
snowflake to reveal a pattern.

Love knocks with such frosted fingers.
I look out. In the shadow
of so vast a God I shiver, unable
to detect the child for the whiteness.

Anybody's Alphabet

All art is anonymous.
Listen: *Ai ee; ai ee,*
the unaspirated sound
out of a cave in anticipation
of human anguish, aftermath
of the alibis of God.

Beauty and the beast
bedded together, begotten
in one womb, battering
later at truth's bars,
beseeching precedence, both
badly bruised in the end.

Compulsion and choice,
contending champions;
co-respondents in a case
not for the courts;
curious as to whether free
one can be compelled to choose.

Dust and decay,
ditherers upon the doorstep
of death itself; dried-
up ghosts of daisy-chain
days that were once dappled
with dew and delight.

Except, then,
for electricity each
of us would be earthed
and effete, our light

like the evening star extinguished
for ever aeons ago.

For Stevens fictions
were as familiar
as facts and if far-
fetched preferable.
Forfeiting for faith
fable, he feasted on it.

God graven
erstwhile gives now
before mind's groping
after him among germs,
galaxies. Gone, he still
gazes upon us. Gracious.

As in Holland
on the horizontal hills
have to be conceived,
so heaven and hell
are hearsay only for those
held up half-way between.

The I as idea
incarnate, inimical
to the impartial, infinite
in the intensity of its
opposition to the incursions
of an implicit Thou.

Is not the judgment
of judicious men
that words beginning
with just j like jeering,

joking all of them put
the jewel-like spirit in jeopardy?

Kingly but not kind:
nature with its knowledge
of how to keep kith
and kin ready to kneel
down or keel over
at the dropping of its kerchief.

Lust and love, the mind's
Siamese twins
listening to each other
lying about life,
one leering, one laughing
in their loneliness together.

Maiden of many
motions, mahogany-
eyed, making with those same
movements as much
music for me as does
your mouth with its modes.

Needing to be neither
narrow nor nasty
to understand how
the neutrality of nice
men is not so much
non-combatant as it is naive.

Overtures of opportunity
or obsequies of the outworn?
Obols are obsolete now
for the oarsman through space-time;

the oracle not so much
out of order as it is out of date.

Particle physics provides
parallels with the Upanishads.
Today's prophet is preoccupied
with the present, that non-
point at which a paradoxical
future paves the way to the past.

In queenlier times
the quaint was the known quantity
the knight was in quest of.
In the age of the quark
the queer's quandary is
that he is not quite.

Is it right for the wrong
to be rich even if
ruefully? Are the real
rewards of romance
to be reaped only when reason
at long last is at rest?

Where is sincerity's sanction?
Six times out of seven
the slippery tongue is successful.
Blake's saying is a sure
stumbling block for simpletons
on their way to salvation.

True to type travelling
towards truth and turning
too often aside.
There are the thoroughfare

and the thousands of
no-through-roads which we take.

Universal understanding
unveiled. Unnecessary
anymore for the under-privileged,
the under-dog to sit up
and beg in the face of usury's
urge towards urbanisation.

Virtually a virgin.
Very well. But veering
towards vagueness, if questioned
on the value of the voluptuous
when no more than a veil
for the viciousness of a virago.

Windy and wet, and what is
worse the weather within
wicked: wounds and the heart's
woe, when all should be well.
Ah, waif spirit, will you not wake
once again to wonder and worship?

The xtremities of the Cross
so far xaggerated
as to become the kiss
of the xploiter, an xample
of how, when all things could
be xcellent, all are wrong.

You and I God – Yahweh,
the scientist's yogi –
youthful as tomorrow;
yawing but never yielding

to my yearning all these years
for myself to become you.

But east of Zion
there is Zen, that zone
where zeal can become
zest. On zany thermometers
then, the readings of the zeitgeist
are never at zero.

Unpublished Poems

Trio

'Brother electricity
ply your shears, work
your fuses to the bone.

Sister water dance
in the sunlight, rub
your girlish sides against rock.

Little children
of the germ cells, genes,
chromosomes, honour the code.'

So sang the mad
giant; and I,
who was sane, ran

hither and thither
among fornicating
millions like a woman

at a fair in
search of her one son
yammering: 'Where has love gone?'

'It is here,' I cry,
'in the hand that daily
makes its incision
into the divine body
from which there flow forth
both tears and money,
that last sacrament in the upper
room of an industrial culture.'

It is the one free act
of the human, a kind of waving
before it goes down under
the material tide, bidding the dove
come with such straws of forgiveness
as are unavailable to the machine.

We will out-computer it.
We will be at the end
of the sentence before it has started.
We will breed from language
prodigies of computation
that will gather at the crossways
of thought and deed. The masterpieces
wait on the future's acknowledgement
we will be in at the kill,
when the god who has given us the slip,
since we began thinking,
is run to earth again in a synapse.
The music of the chromosones
will be ours. 'Take your partners'
we will say 'for the dance
that will outlast the second
law of thermodynamics.' The nuclear

explosion gives birth to a fireball
that will survive the passing
of our tubercular sun.

Easter

Easter. I go to church
to proclaim with my fellows:
I believe in the Resurrection –
of what? Here everything
is electric and automatic.
In April a myriad bulbs
are switched on as flowers
incandesce; a new generation
of creatures rehearses
its genetic code. All this is easy.
Earth is a self-regulating
machine; everything happens
because it must. My faith
is in the inevitability
of creation. There will come a day –
dust under a dry sun,
ashes under its incineration . . .
is there somewhere in all
the emptiness of the universe
a fertile star where the old
metaphors will apply, where
the bugling daffodil will sound
abroad not the last post, but
a gush of music out of an empty tomb?

Alaska

Out here there is no history;
the cliff's withered face
is too weathered to be human.

The sky is a blank lens;
photographs that the inlet
had taken were never developed.

If people there are
they keep themselves to
themselves, so there are no harbours.

Somewhere a bough cracks,
a stone drops, but the conifers stand
perpetually to attention.

If only there were a tale
here; some maiden pining,
pouring her hair in a slow fall

between the sunset
and the first star. Emptiness
only and silence,

and the interior frowning.
God's commandment: Be fruitful
and multiply was revised

here. The only mathematics
is the sum the centuries
are at work upon, never

to be finished. I sink
to my knees, visitor to a temple
God has abandoned,

asking a reason for
this unending anthem to which
no one is listening. There is no answer.

The Shadow

At times there is this shadow
falling across our path,
projected by no substance.

It is the original
anonymity, that leaves presents
on so many doorsteps,

or makes casualties happen
in so fortuitous a manner
that there is nobody to blame.

There is a game it plays
in which, when it appears
to be furthest off, then is it

most close. It entices us
up and up the twin-sided
helix only to abandon us

thirsty beside the gene pool.
It is the one we wrestle with
and are thrown with no

stigmata to display as proof
of the encounter. There is an invitation
we receive, standing outside

the laboratory of the self,
either to go in
and have everything explained

or take mystery by the hand
and be led faltering towards the love
that is at the centre of its withdrawing.

Pause

'Rest a while,'
        says the muse,
but I press on
        losing myself between
the dictionary and the blank
        page. Wisdom advises,
'Call her bluff and
        she'll come cringing.'
But I am all nerves,
        running vocabulary
through my fingers, faster
        and faster. And somewhere
before me is
        the great poem, wrapped
in its stillness, that
        I fool myself into
thinking I will overtake soon
        by putting on speed.

Wisdom

Those days I was wise.
I knew by the scarecrow
in the arable that a god
had been there. It is
by rags that we attain
to the divine. It is on our knees
we advance furrow by furrow
to such charity as there is.
To me in those days
every tree was a cross
from which love had come down
to work with us in the soil
until the tree blossomed.
Stones thrown into a bucket
were no harder than the prayers
we bruised our spirits upon,
scrabbling among those acres.
It was the wrong deliverance
I sought for. The dark angel
came and showed me a light
that was artificial. The machine
fondled and in a moment
the land turned over, purring
with abundance. 'And who
am I to thank for this?'
I enquired, seeing the grass
pouring from the chapel windows,
hearing the tractor's mockery
of the dead choirs. 'You have
nobody to congratulate
but yourself' replied science,

spraying me with its own sunlight,
while the weather vane on the church
tower pointed in a direction
no-one had ever imagined existed before.

Her Smile

Always her eyes
unable to close
lest death should steal
up on her unawares.
Oh, not from fear, but
because she had things
to arrange: friends,
her friends, unfriendly
with one another, to be made
friendly once more; a family
to be re-assured by her
pretending she was immortal.

Seeing those small bones,
her breath a butterfly
endeavouring to escape her;
her eyes wounded
by failures of taste
never to be mentioned,
I gave my wrath rein
only to see how
it was brought up short,
trembling but becoming
quiet again under
the stroking of her infirm smile.

Butterfly Movement

Butterfly movement
as though a rainbow
had taken wing, falling
with the softness of light

on our horizon, a reminder
of God's promise to lay
aside wrath. And what,
this moment at gaze

in the afternoon sun,
we ask, was the nature
of our sin that it deserved
so beautifully to be forgiven?

Robin

Dawn. The robin
crumbles his song
into a few pieces
for our Communion.
And humbly we accept;
we need the sacrament
of the Real Presence
if we are to continue
to believe. Pure
spirit is a refraction
only. It is the rainbow
in life's spray that,
when we put our starved hand
into, lets our hand through.

But this wafer of song
we touch with the tip
of our belief, is it not
the pearl without price
we were told of and
have come upon that
we must give up all
our payments on a hire-purchase
happiness to make our own?

Back from Dubai

In competition with nothing
            but a star,
holding it in its bill
like an offering to April . . .
            All this, God,
in eternity's back garden
listening to a blackbird.
what, then, of the cloudy
sierras, the cloudless
            savannahs? Did you
inveigle him out, that first man
with wings, offering him
            the blue, unreachable
apple on horizonless branches?
            When I thought
I was going up, I was going
out to join the dancers
about a serene vortex.
Where, then, was the song
            of the blackbird
among the epicycles
of space-time with the OM
of creation issuing
            from a packed hive?
How fall to prayer with nothing
to kneel on? Why shield my eyes
from a light that was already
            within me?
Out there on my own
had I come like Actaeon

on the naked, unapproachable truth
with nowhere to hide, being changed
      from hunter to quarry,
amid all that inhospitable
blue, from its pursuing fury?

Resurrection

Easter. The grave clothes of winter
are still here, but the sepulchre
is empty. A messenger
from the tomb tells us
how a stone has been rolled
from the mind, and a tree lightens
the darkness with its blossom.
There are travellers upon the roads
who have heard music blown
from a bare bough, and a child
tells us how the accident
of last year, a machine stranded
beside the way for lack
of petrol is covered with flowers.

Dusk

Night that to the stars
says 'Open', to other
flowers, to this lily
in particular, says:
'Shut'. I was in bud
once, clenched on
a thought, until day
dawned, peeled back
my petals; I was all
stamen. Love came to me
for my pollen, made
honey in a brief
comb. Was it a day,
a year? Night that has
kept its distance,
that says to the blossom
in a dark orchard
'Open', says now
to me here 'Close'.

How?

How shall we sing the Lord's song
in the land of the electron,
of the micro-chip? Are these also
ingredients of a divinity
we have been educated to misunderstand?
Our dependence on him is anticipated
by our expertise. Since our prayers
are material, we let the computer
say our Amens for us. We enter
our banks as we would a cathedral,
listening to the yen singing
and the other currencies accompanying
it in Esperanto. In a universe
that is expanding our theologies
have contracted. We reduce
the God-man to the human, the human
to the machine, watching it demolish
forests faster than we can grow even
one tree of faith for our Saviour to come down from.

Two Views of a Gorilla

We confront one another,
a meeting not of minds
but of fingers. Is it sadness
I imagine on his gnarled
face, sadness for failure
to catch up; sadness rather
for what I have become,
a brother who has put him
behind bars, when all he asks
of me is that I love him?
When two such contemplate
each other, which is made monster
by the bars that are between them?

Dying, she put out a finger
in my direction; trembling
I touched it. The gorilla
postponing the death of the species
behind bars, puts out a hand, too,
which I take, putting the stars
in a frenzy. All over the night
sky their alarm rings,
warning of the danger
that, in all the emptiness
around, when two creatures
meet, they can come so close
via the emotions to meaning.

Montserrat

Sometimes taking advantage
of the low cloud God drew near
the wall-eyed and the heavy
of hearing, so that a shudder ran
through the alcoves and the cloisters,
and prayers that had kept him at bay
ages yielded and he stole in,
appearing like phosphorescence
in the confessionals, like living dust
at the nostrils that for so long
had suffered an asthma of the spirit.
Brothers who had not raised their heads
in years from their breviaries
whispered in unison their Amens,
as the light winced at his passing,
while far back in the chapel
choristers who had been whitening
through the dark night of the soul
turned, all of them, golden a moment
as though their voices were thawed flame.

The Price

Part of an inscrutable
economy, where one voice
is not heard above another
voice, but all are engaged
on the work they were programmed
to address, bringing man's
shining pinnacles to the ground,
gorging themselves among the ruins.
Up and down in their world
is without meaning. All
they know is to use man's
altitude to bring him down.
Invisibly they migrate
from casualty to casualty,
disparaging the filters, inaudibly
singing the canticles of their kind.
These God found reconnoitring
the frontier between the live
and the dead forms and took his place
on the Cross, high over
the starved eyes and the clenched fists,
willing to pay indemnities of the heart
for an intellectual indecision.

The Spectator

I sit in the window
and am sad. Is it because Europe
is spread out before me? The promises, the ruins?
I see the armies marching
to extinction. The words of the prophets
are applauded and disobeyed.
It was a wise painter kept his brushes
from going bald, a wiser composer
left his symphony unfinished.
The inventor looks into a bottomless
glass and is in no way abstemious.
The periods promenade by
and are too fast for my camera.
Was that Athens, the Quatrocento,
Louis Quatorze? The computer flickers
and goes out as another meteorite
heads our way. The path to Calvary
is eroded by a mechanical
impatience. Is there a grant
still to be had for the upkeep
of a cross with the god-man
rotting upon it, his head bowed
under an irradiated halo?

Poems in Flight

Brushed ever so lightly
by a poem's passing. Got it,
missed. The poem goes
its way with the rest,
with nowhere to go
but back to the vocabulary
from which it set off.
I wish there were a migration
time for poetry, so nets
could be set up in promising
places. No luck. Poems
have no call-notes, nor have they
set times. They come from where
they have been wintering, seeking
for places in which to fashion
the words' nest, high in the boughs
of thought or deep down
in impenetrable darkness.
There are no trappers
of a poem. We only know
when one is about when it has drifted
by us, trailing a fragrance.

Index of Titles

Index of Titles

Index of First Lines